I PLAYED
AND
I WON

To

Ronnie James

God Bless You

Al Worthington

I PLAYED AND I WON

THE AL WORTHINGTON STORY

WITH V. BEN KENDRICK

xulon
PRESS

I Played And I Won, The Al Worthington Story
by Allan Worthington

Printed in the United States of America

Library of Congress Control Number: 2004096789

ISBN 1-594677-88-3

www.xulonpress.com

ACKNOWLEDGMENT

I want to express my appreciation to those who helped in the production of this book. I thank my brother, Charles, for providing some insights of our family's home life. I also give thanks to my wife, Shirley, and to Nina Kendrick for their proofreading. Thanks to Linda J. White for arranging and typing the manuscript.

My special thanks to Dr. V. Ben Kendrick for his many hours of research and writing to make this book possible. His regular communications with me during the course of his work on the manuscript is greatly appreciated.

Permission granted for use of all pictures

TABLE OF CONTENTS

REFLECTIONS

FOREWORD

Few persons have influenced me as deeply as Al Worthington. My first experience with this burly, menacing, unshaven right handed pitcher occurred in the old Polo Grounds in 1957 when "Big Red" took the mound for the New York Giants and faced a trembling rookie infielder at bat for the Chicago Cubs – me. His fastball was "alive," his slider sharp, and his control uncertain. But it was his attitude toward me, the hitter that unnerved me. Al Worthington was mean!

The next time I faced Al was across the coffee table in he and wife Shirley's apartment in Phoenix during spring training in 1960. A Christian radio station in Minneapolis, KTIS, had asked me to tape an interview with Al, now a star pitcher with the San Francisco Giants. He was clean-shaven now and his attitude was one of kindness, concern, and genuine friendliness. Why and how the dramatic change in my reaction to this big, smiling, soft-spoken native of Alabama? Al Worthington had met Jesus Christ!

Al went on to describe that afternoon in Phoenix how, with several Giant teammates; he had been talked into attending the Billy Graham Crusade held in San Francisco in the fall of 1958. At the conclusion of Graham's gospel message that evening, he faithfully issued an invitation to those in the vast audience who wanted to respond to God's offer of a new life in Christ, to come forward in repentance and faith and make a public stand. And thus began Al Worthington's journey with Jesus.

That journey is beautifully described in this inspiring autobiography: from Big League stardom to minor league obscurity; from World Series cheers to scorn and ridicule from teammates; from weakness and compromise to integrity and righteousness; from banishment and dismissal to praise and redemption.

One of God's great blessings to me has been the two years Al Worthington and I were roommates on the 1964 and 1965

Minnesota Twins. He taught and challenged me to be faithful in prayer, bold in witnessing, dependant on Scripture, and steadfast in service to Christ. It is Al's example in the above that influences me to this very day.

As you read this book, you will be struck, perhaps for the first time, by the truth of God's promises revealed in the Bible, His Holy Word. I particularly commend you to two of these eternal truths.

"O keep my soul, and deliver me: let me not be ashamed; for I put my trust in thee. Let integrity and uprightness preserve me; for I wait on thee." (Psalm 25:20,21) – The Prayer of David.

"Therefore, my beloved brethren, be ye steadfast, unmovable, always abounding in the work of the Lord, forasmuch as ye know that your labor is not in vain in the Lord." (I Corinthians 15:58) – The Apostle Paul.

This is the life story of a man who sought, first of all, to be exalted in the world's eyes through success in major league baseball. Instead, through the grace of God, Al Worthington discovered a better way! (I Peter 5:6,7).

Jerry Kindall
Head Baseball Coach (retired)
University of Arizona

INTRODUCTION

I have known Al Worthington through his early years in baseball as an outstanding pitcher but even more for his bold witness for our Lord Jesus. I batted against him and knew him as a relief specialist and a fierce competitor.

And then on a university level, we coached together at Liberty University where he molded the baseball team to compete as a Division I team. They named the baseball complex in his honor. I followed him as Athletic Director and his legacy at Liberty continues.

Just as in Major League baseball, Al had a tremendous impact on those around him. His zeal for witnessing will assure that many will spend eternity in heaven because he very tactfully presented a personal relationship with a living Savior.

This book, through his dry wit, will challenge all who read it.

Bobby Richardson
Former New York Yankee Second Baseman

DEDICATION

I dedicate this book to my wonderful wife, Shirley, and to our children. First of all, to Shirley who has stood with me for 53 years and who has been a real helpmate. Her role as mother has been a priority for her. I am proud of Shirley.

Second, our children have been my best fans and friends. I am grateful for them and am proud to be their father.

Linda, our oldest is age 52. She has four children and all are God-fearing. She is a godly woman and a dedicated mother. Linda was saved at age eight. She has a very sweet personality and relates well to people.

Al is our eldest son and second child. Perhaps his greatest asset is his love for his wife and children. He is an exceptional dad to Allison and Justin. When he was age seven, he accepted Jesus as his Savior. In my opinion he is the best dad that I know.

Michele is our third child and second daughter. She is now 46 years old. Michele was saved at age six in our living room after Sunday dinner. She and Ernie serve the Lord in a Christian school. Michele has multiple talents that she uses for the Lord.

Marshal is a very humble person who is dedicated to his wife, Susan and children, as well as to the Lord. He has what I call a political flair. He was age five when his Sunday school teacher asked everyone to close their eyes and then asked what they saw. She answered by saying there was nothing but darkness. That is what hell is like except for the light from the fire. Marshal came home and got saved.

Daniel who is 14 months younger than Marshal, has always been the funny one of the family. He is an adventurous person. Daniel thrives in living on the edge. He is very generous and thoughtful in his giving. He loves life. Daniel was saved at age four.

As of this writing, Shirley and I have eleven wonderful grandchildren ranging from 29 years old to one year old. What a joy! Our children have tender hearts toward God. None of them

have given us any problems. It is wonderful the way God has
blessed our home. Bless His Holy Name.

Al Worthington

1

NEWCOMER FROM FULTON SPRINGS

The roar of the crowd sounded more like 30,000 instead of the 6,650 paying customers who were there to see their beloved New York Giants play the Philadelphia Phillies.

On the mound in the famous horseshoe shaped Polo Grounds, with its background stage of Coogan's Bluff, was rookie Allan Fulton Worthington. He had never played in a double deck stadium before and he mentioned later that he was a bit nervous and scared. The fans radiated their excitement. Al, with just two and one half years of minor league ball behind him, was pitching his first major league game. The big 24 year-old right-hander, standing six feet two inches tall with 205 pounds spread over his muscular frame was about to close the door on the Phillies. The newcomer to manager Leo Durocher's pitching staff had a no hitter going until the Phillies' catcher, Smokey Burgess, doubled to the left field corner in the fifth inning.

"Get control of yourself," Al said to himself after hard-hitting Del Ennis, the Phils' left fielder, drew the fourth walk of the game after two were out in the ninth inning. With Ennis on first, right fielder Johnny Wyrostek hit a ground ball through the right side of the infield into right field for another double. Ennis stopped at third base. "Come on, Connie, bring them in," yelled someone from the dugout, as Connie Ryan strolled to the plate.

Ryan came into the game in the seventh as a pinch runner for Earl Torgeson and stayed to play first base. "I wanted each pitch to be the one that would seal the game for the Giants," said Al.

The big hurler stared hard and long at his veteran battery mate, Wes Westrum. He glanced at Ennis who was lengthening his lead from third base. The right-hander fired the ball to the plate. Ryan swung and bounced the ball back to Al. He grabbed it and threw the ball to first baseman Whitey Lockman for the third out and the ballgame.

The fans erupted with excitement. Not only was there a celebration on the field and later in the clubhouse but unknown to the cheering happy fans in the Polo Grounds, there was another celebration in Birmingham, Alabama, at 4109 38th Avenue North where Al's 83 year old grandmother, Mrs. Lucy Worthington, was gathered around a radio with grandchildren and great grandchildren. Al's parents, Walter and Lake Worthington, were visiting their daughter, Mildred, in Miami, Florida, during the time of their son's sensational performance in the shadow of Coogan's Bluff. When Al was asked about his accomplishment, he said, "It was the best game I have pitched in my life. I used mostly a fastball. I threw only four curve balls, and not until late in the game."

Philadelphia manager, Steve O'Neill, commented about Al saying, "He showed the poise of a veteran on the mound."

Accolades of praise, written and vocal, were coming from every corner of the baseball world. Hall of Famer, Dizzy Dean, one half of the famous Dean brothers duo, Dizzy and Daffy, said this about the new comer to the Giants' pitching staff, "Where have they been hiding this guy? He has a zigzag fast ball, a good low slider, a nice easy motion and lets the ball go just at the right time. I hope nobody gets the idea of teaching him something. You don't play around with natural pitchers like this kid."

Leo Durocher, the controversial but well respected Giants manager said, "I'm convinced the kid's got it. He's got everything – fastball, curve and control, and cool as an ice cube. What a difference he'll make!" In an added comment, Durocher summed up his thoughts about Al and his phenomenal major league debut by saying, "Great, great, great." Cy Perkins, a coach for the Phillies, and former catcher for 17 years with the Philadelphia Athletics, New York Yankees, and Detroit Tigers, had this to say about the young pitcher, "The kid looked like Walter Johnson out there."

With the baseball media focusing on Al because of his two hit shutout in his first major league appearance, life was anything but calm for him.

Shirley, his attractive bride of three years didn't even have the privilege of watching her husband become famous. She was still with her parents in Fulda, Minnesota, where Al had taken her before reporting to the Giants. She finally arrived in New York on Friday, July 10, five days after Al's starting performance against Philadelphia and the day before Al was scheduled to pitch against the heavy hitting Brooklyn Dodgers in their home park, Ebbets Field. Shirley told of her arrival in the big city and why she did not go to Brooklyn. Referring to the game, she said, "That was in Brooklyn. I'm only a small town girl and I was afraid of making that long trip alone." Shirley and two-year old daughter, Linda, were in a three-room Manhattan apartment in Washington Heights.

The apartment was made available to them when Bill Connelly was sent to the Minneapolis Millers' triple A club in the American Association to make room for Al on the Giants' roster. The apartment was not only home for Al, Shirley, and baby Linda, but also served as a needed place of refuge. They were a close-knit family.

Shirley's faithful support of Al and being a constant source of encouragement greatly added to the diamond successes of her fast becoming famous husband.

"I could not have had any greater support than I got from my wife, my parents, Shirley's parents, other members of my family, and my multitude of friends," said Al, beaming with his natural smile. "I am very fortunate to have such a wonderful family. I thank God for each one of them."

Describing his trip to Brooklyn with Sal Maglie and Jim Hearn, Al related, "As I rode over to Brooklyn, I knew I was pitching that day and I like to have jumped out of the car realizing I was to pitch against that Dodger lineup. I was out of my league."

The two pitcher teammates riding with Al were no slouches when it came to beating opposing teams. Sal Maglie, known affectionately as the Barber, racked up a total of 41 wins the last two seasons. He was greatly respected for his pitching skills from those who faced him from the batter's box. He was the best one to give tips to Al on the Brooklyn hitters. The Barber was known as a Dodger Killer. He seemed to have what it took to beat the Brooklyn Bums, as their faithful followers knew them.

Jim Hearn was also a good source to give Al tips. The preceding two years, 1951-52, he racked up 31 wins for the Giants. When Al was asked if any of the veteran players on the Giants were a help and encouragement to him, he responded without hesitation, "All the veteran players on the Giants were helpful. They were class men and not afraid to give you advice even if you took their job."

Al, Sal and Jim arrived at Ebbets Field, the home of the Dodgers from 1913-1957. Once on the field, Al stood and stared at the ballpark he had never before seen. Players, who were just names before, were now warming up taking batting practice, catching fungo flies hit to the outfield, playing catch, and running short dashes. The young pitcher felt challenged as he watched sluggers like Duke Snyder, Roy Campanella, Gil Hodges, and Jackie Robinson drive the baseballs over the screen in right field and into the stands in left and center.

He finally had his first look at the powerful Dodger team that had hit one or more home runs extending their streak to 24 games in a row. They were one game away from tying the all time record of the 1941 New York Yankees.

The call, "Play ball" came from home plate Umpire Engeln. The 22,642-mixed crowd of Dodgers and Giants fans loudly cheered for their respective team. Those in the front box seats were close to the playing field. It was Dodgers' broadcaster, Red Barber, who said that the people who sat in the box seats were so close they were practically infielders.

Unknown to the 24-year-old rookie, history was about to be made in the game between the cross-town archrivals. The Giants, in the first inning, gave Al a three run cushion. Left fielder, Monte Irvin, belted one of Russ Meyers' offerings into the centerfield seats to put the Giants up three to nothing.

"Ok, big guy, show them your stuff," said one of Al's teammates as they left the dugout to take the field.

Stuck close to her radio was fan number one, Shirley Worthington, in Manhattan. Other family members in Alabama, and Shirley's family in Minnesota were also glued to their radios. As each of the Dodgers took their turn at bat, they found it hard to believe that this young, little-experienced pitcher was mowing them down with ease. He retired the first ten batters before Pewee Reese, the Dodger Captain, worked him for a walk in the fourth inning.

Powerful hitter, Duke Snyder, strolled to the plate and spoiled Al's no hitter by sending a single to right field. Peewee played it safe, stopping at second base. Dodger catcher, Roy Campanella, took his wide spread stance in the batters box. The stocky future Hall of Famer promptly bounced into a double play cutting off Brooklyn's threat.

"You're doing great, Al" said someone from the end of the bench as Al entered the dugout. "Thanks," replied Al who was still getting to know his new teammates. "I'm trying to keep it down to them," he added as he took his place on the bench. The Dodgers were helpless before the pitching of the rookie right-hander. Their scouting reports on young Al declared that he would not tire, and he didn't! The game ended sending the Flatbush faithful home wondering who this Worthington kid was and why hadn't they heard about him before.

"Congratulations, Al; Great game, Kid; Nice pitching, Partner," were a few of the remarks said to Al from the excited teammates who crowded around the new pitching star. He not only shut out the Dodgers 6 – 0, but he only gave them four hits and all were singles.

For the second time within the space of a week, the sports writers across the country and around the world were searching the record books and sending forth praises for the little known new Giant pitcher, Allan Fulton Worthington.

Shirley, along with the far spread Worthington and Reusse (Shirley's family) families; were yelling, crying, hugging and laughing, over the unbelievable accomplishment of their beloved Al.

The famous new-comer to the Giants set a modern National League record by pitching shutouts in his first two major league starts. He never pitched a ball in a Major League game before he faced the Phillies the previous Monday.

In addition to his record setting, he had pitched 18 scoreless innings winning his first two games with twin showings, 6 – 0 against the Phillies and Dodgers. He also made it eight wins in a row for the Giants, which gave them a big boost in their pennant hopes.

It must have been a very humbling experience to the heavy hitting Brooklyn Club to have been shut out for the first time that year by an unknown kid pitcher who had just two and one half years in professional baseball.

"To say that Al made a big splash is putting it mildly," said a baseball fan, "he opened the flood gates on the Phillies and Brooklyn."

The ride back to Manhattan was a joyful time for the two veteran pitchers and their new friend and Dodger Killer, Al Fulton Worthington. The three-team mates talked non-stop about the game in Brooklyn. "You did a good job of keeping the ball low," said Sal Maglie to Al. "In fact, you didn't pitch a ball above the knees." The Barber had to be correct in what he told Al because there were only seven balls hit to the outfield the entire game.

They dropped Al off at his apartment where he found Shirley bubbling with excitement. Her Al had just pitched one of the finest games of his career no matter how many years it would last.

Al tells the story about his brother, Charles, who was in the Navy and was stationed in Japan. One of the sailors, who knew his brother, was listening to Armed Forces Network and the Game of the Day. He heard the name, Worthington, who was pitching for the Giants against the Dodgers. He immediately went and found Al's brother, Charles. He told him, "There is a Worthington pitching. Is he any relation to you?" Charles said, "No." Al gets a laugh out of the story every time he tells it. Charles knew that Allan was in professional baseball at the minor league level but he had not heard that he was elevated to the majors. He didn't think that Al was good enough to be up there. Al's two hit, 6 – 0 win over the Philadelphia Phillies on July 5, 1953 and his four hit, 6 – 0 win over the Brooklyn Dodgers five days later raised a lot of eyebrows and generated countless conversations in the baseball world.

Fans from far and near were asking where the new Giants' pitcher came from and why had they not heard about him before. There is much to say about this young baseball star and how God had His hand upon him from his early childhood days.

2

CLOSE BRUSH WITH DEATH

Walter and Lake Worthington were a couple that took marriage seriously. They were committed to each other for life and their devotion and love for each other were clearly seen by their ten children. The young couple started their family in Fulton Springs, a rural area, just north of Birmingham, Alabama.

Walter was the first-born followed by Mildred. After Mildred came Evelynn, Robert Oliver, Dorothy, Betty, Allan, Mary Alice, Charles and last of all Edna Earle.

After the birth of Edna Earle, the family moved into Birmingham. Within a period of five years the Worthington family moved several times but finally settled into a five room house in Inglenook, a small community nearby, and remained there until all the children were grown.

On February 5, 1929, a baby boy was born to Walter and Lake Worthington. There was no hospital delivery for the seventh child in the Worthington household. In talking about his birth, Al said, "I was told that I was born in our home located in Fulton Springs. Maybe my mama could not think of another name to give me so I was stuck with Fulton for my middle name. My first name, Allan is all right but the name Fulton never seemed to fit me. The only way I can accept it is because my dear mama gave it to me. We kids had a wonderful mother and father.

My brother, Charles, in writing about our mother, describes her as 'love in action' that was what she truly was to all of us. In his writing about our family, he mentioned the hard years of the depression and World War II which helped bind our family together in a unity of love and caring for one another."

In reminiscing about his childhood days, Al spoke of his first remembrances: He said, "The first thing I can remember was pulling myself up on the rocking chair that pop was sitting in on the porch of our house at Fulton Springs. I also remember mama making us chocolate pudding and bringing it outside to us. I have mostly good memories of my boyhood days.

I'll never forget stepping on a nail. One of the things I remember so well was bathing in the tub of water which mama carried from a well down the street. There are so many things that come to mind once I start thinking about my early days as a boy."

Al laughed when he told the story about a pair of shoes he had to wear. "It happened when I was in the fifth grade. Walter's wife, Elizabeth, my sister-in-law, went to town and bought Mary Alice a pair of shoes for $2.00. That was very nice of Elizabeth to do that for Mary Alice but when Elizabeth brought them home, they were too big for Mary Alice's feet. The next thing I knew, I was given the shoes to try on. The shoes were too small and hurt my little toes. Somebody got the idea to make slits on the side of the shoes to give more room for my little toes. The next day, I wore my new shoes to school even though they pinched my feet. I walked around the back of the school to avoid being seen but ran into some of my friends. They immediately spotted the shoes and began to laugh. They were poor like we were but seeing me in girl's shoes was funny to them. It was embarrassing to me but I have to admit, it was funny."

One day Al overheard his oldest brother, Walter, talking to his mother. "Mama," said Walter holding his shotgun on his shoulder, "put the pot on. I'm going to bring some squirrels back for supper." Another thing that Al remembers well when he was going to grammar school, "It was during recess time one day and we were having a lot of fun wrestling," grinned Al as he told the story. "I was one of the bigger boys in school and usually won my matches. It was easy for me to take on two or three of my classmates and put them on the ground. I was big and strong for my age.

Not liking to be beaten all the time, one of the boys went and told the teacher that I had said a bad word. Without any investigation into what had happened, she made me stand looking toward the sun with my mouth open. She told me that I had to hold my mouth open so the sun would clean my tongue. It was not a nice experience for me but I believe the principle involved is good."

"Our home was a wonderful place," said Al. "We didn't have much of this world's goods but we did have a mother and father who loved us and did what they could to provide for us. My older sisters always worked at odd jobs helping to support themselves and the family.

Lack of material things never seemed to bother any of us. My brother, Charles, wrote a family background which describes our family relationship with each other and early events that took place that touched our lives."

Charles in writing of his family background said, "My father was the authoritative figure in the home. Everything seemed to revolve around his schedule, as he often worked different shifts. We were not allowed to begin our meal until he was seated and had offered thanks. My mother seemed to mind him just like the rest of us. He never raised his voice toward her or us; nor do I remember but one instance of their quarreling. However, when he spoke, we listened. Morally, he exemplified the highest standards. He never used profanity, and did not tolerate it in others, either in the home or on the ball field where he was usually found after work. Both friend and foe alike respected him. The only time he would indulge in strong drink was on Christmas Day. He took pride in being the best eggnog maker in the community. After my brothers and I got saved, we stopped drinking Pop's eggnog and he stopped making it anymore.

Although church attendance was part of our upbringing, and some of the older children were actively involved, religion was not one of the major emphasis around our house. Both of my parents joined the church as a young married couple and vowed to raise their children in church. They never broke that vow. Each of us was christened as infants and confirmed at around twelve years of age. Yet, as far as reading the Bible or even discussing the Bible, there was a total absence. Like many people during those days, our faith was in the church. Grace at the table and nighttime prayer is all the prayer that I remember.

My father's main interest in life was sports. He was a printer by trade, and completed only the sixth grade. His father died at an early age and he had to go to work to help support his mother and younger brother. Books or magazines of any kind were virtually absent from our home. As a family, we gathered around the radio in the winter, and played ball the rest of the year. Times were hard and this left little time for intellectual pursuits, even if the desire was there.

Although we loved one another, we had trouble verbalizing it. We got it honestly from both our parents. My dad's idea of affection was to hold you on his lap and rub his whiskers across your face or grab your thigh and squeeze it tightly, showing how a "horse bites". We weren't much better. We could muster up a handshake, but that would be about all. We knew that we loved one another, but couldn't say it. Pride accounted for most of our lack of affection. We were poor (so were most in our community), but proud. Even though we might have learned these traits from our dad, we still wouldn't trade him for anyone else. It was years later, however, before some of us came to this realization. His moral principles and strength of character will forever be cherished.

Like my father, my mother too, was not much on affection. She lost her mother at an early age and was raised by a stepmother and four older stepbrothers and sisters. She was neither a sports fan nor a leader. She did not particularly like public events, even though she always attended with her family. She loved her home and was always too busy washing, ironing, and cleaning to consider outside work. As children growing up, we always had the assurance that mama would be home when we arrived from school. She never interfered or took our side when daddy was correcting us. In all her actions, she thought only of others.

Unknowingly, my parents practiced many biblical principles. One of these was that of mental and physical health. My parents never believed in acknowledging sickness or failure, or giving in to either. If we were sick and complained, we were told that they (parents) were the doctors. If we continued to complain, we were given a dose of castor oil or milk of magnesia. We soon learned to take care of our own illnesses and to keep quiet about it. My dad also taught us not to harbor wrong thoughts, and to push on regardless of the circumstances. It paid off for him as he never missed but a few days from work due to illness in over 55 years."

Not many of Allan's fans know of his close brush with death when he was a young child. It was early in the spring of 1935. Little Allan was six years old. Because of cramped quarters, Allan and Oliver shared the same bed. Oliver knew that something was wrong because of the strange way his brother was talking. He went to tell his parents. "Mama," Oliver said nervously, "something is wrong with Allan. He's talking out of his head." The doctor was called and came to the Worthington house. Allan's brothers and sisters knew that whatever was wrong with their brother; it must be serious to call the doctor. It didn't seem very long before Dr. Argo, who had his office in nearby Boyles, arrived at the Worthington home on Hale Avenue in Inglenook.

"I'm sorry to tell you, Mr. and Mrs. Worthington but Allan has double pneumonia." Said Dr. Argo with a worried look on his face." You know that I will do all that I can for him." In telling about his serious illness years later, Al commented, "There was little known at that time about pneumonia. In fact, many of the afflicted died."

Little Allan was moved to the front bedroom that had two windows. The windows were open from the top and bottom

13

twenty-four hours of the day. The room was purposely kept cold. His body was propped up with pillows so he could breathe. A kettle containing water and medication sat on a nearby hot plate. Allan inhaled the vapor, which helped him to breathe easier. "We had wonderful neighbors," said Al speaking of his sickness. "There were Polly Kelly, the Harveys, the Rives, Mac Anderson, who was a nurse, the Bryants, and the Keiths. Mac, the nurse, was in and out day and night. She was a jewel if ever there was one. Food was brought in from the neighbors. Everybody was so wonderful." Dr. Argo's wife said that he prayed every morning and every night for the six-year old child.

Even the town's authorities showed concern for little Allan. The street was blocked off because Al could not stand any noise. All visitors entered the house by way of the back door. Sisters Betty and Dorothy stayed with Mrs. Bryant, a neighbor. Their older sister, Mildred, cared for Mary Alice, Charles and Edna Earle. Near the house was a railroad track and the railroad workers would stop on the bridge and talk about the sick little boy. Sometimes, they would knock on the back door to inquire about Allan. There was a light on in the house all night. As long as the light was on; the neighbors knew little Allan was still alive. There was always someone at his bedside.

The six-year old continued to fail in health. One Saturday, Oliver was playing basketball at a nearby Catholic Church. He came running home with a pin that Priest Rafferty sent to be pinned on Allan's nightshirt. The priest said that he would burn candles and pray all night for Allan. The Methodist Church where Walter and Lake were members had a nurse who needed work. The minister, Rev. Baker, offered a suggestion to the concerned parents. "As you no doubt know," he began, "Miss Smith of our church family is a nurse and at the present time, does not have work. If it is alright with you folks, she could help out with Allan at night and the church would pay her." The thankful parents gladly accepted Rev. Baker's suggestion.

Hope was fading for Allan. He was described as a tiny skeleton propped up on pillows. The little lad was so weak and helpless yet fought hard to live. Neighbors washed the family's laundry.

One day when Allan was suffering with a lot of pain, Mac Henderson, the nurse, came in and diagnosed the problem immediately. She straddled Al and pressed on his stomach to expel the accumulative gas. He struggled through the night. The morning light brought no hope for the frail skinny boy. The final hours for Allan seemed to be rapidly approaching. Dr. Argo arrived bringing with him, Dr. Lineberry, a specialist from Norwood Hospital. The room was very quiet.

"According to medical science, we have done everything that we can do for him," said Dr. Lineberry. The specialist with a worried expression looked at Mrs. Worthington sitting in a nearby chair, with her husband standing behind her. The specialist took the mother's hand and said, "Your son is in the hands of a Higher Being." The beloved mother looked at both doctors with eyes filled with tears and with the sound of confidence in her voice, said, "Doctors, he belonged to God before he belonged to me." The room stayed quiet as all eyes gazed upon 'mama' and her sick little boy on the bed.

Before they left, Dr. Argo said, "We are prescribing that Allan be given a teaspoon of whiskey every 15 minutes." "But, Doctor," said Mama, "I don't have any whiskey and besides what will the preacher say?" Dr. Argo replied, "Mrs. Worthington, you are in a railroad community, and someone has some whiskey." Within a short time, whiskey was brought to the Worthington home. Every 15 minutes, the dose of whiskey was given. Someone said that Al's mouth opened like a little bird. The skeleton like boy with his sunken eyes and skin hanging on his bones continued to hold on to life. Homemade mustard plasters along with Vick's salve covered his chest. Dr Argo told Al's parents more than once that he would not make it through the night.

The turning point for Al, of all things, involved a baseball. "I was laying there in the bed listening to some of the neighborhood kids playing baseball across the street. One of them hit the ball, which got lost and they couldn't find it. I could see it, however, from where I was in bed. I hollered as loud as I could, "There it is!" From that time on, I had a great desire to get out and play, which helped me start to get stronger. For eight long weeks, death knocked on my door. How thankful I am, it was only a knock and not an entrance."

Spring arrived in all its beauty. With his skin pulled over his bones and his feet drawn back, Al had to learn to walk all over again. His brothers and sisters pulled him to the community park in a wagon. The wagon had pillows in it so he could lie down if he got tired. His sisters were embarrassed by their brother – a tiny skeleton with a big head. The recovery process was difficult for Al. But after all he had gone through, regaining strength and being able to play outside with his friends presented a real challenge to the lad. Looking back on his sickness, Al said, "It seemed like I went to sleep in the winter and woke up in the spring."

3

INGLENOOK'S RED BIRDS

The dreadful weeks of illness left a lasting scar on Al. Long after that experience, a sound, smell, noise or something he saw would take him back to those seemingly endless days in bed as he lingered between life and death. The smell of a cigar, for example, would remind him of his dad. "When spring came," said Al, "pop would sit on the front porch and smoke a cigar. With the window open, the cigar smoke drifted into my bedroom. I loved the smell of the cigar smoke. Even though we were poor, pop somehow managed to always have a cigar to smoke. We thought pop earned that right. Besides, the smell of the cigar made me feel good. Pop worked hard on a regular basis. A person at the company called one night and said pop had taken ill and someone should come and get him. It was the first time that we children heard of pop missing any work because of illness."

One day during the height of Al's sickness, his father made a promise to him. He wanted so much to see his young son get well, he decided to promise him something that would encourage him to fight even harder to get better. "Allan," said his dad, "When you get over this sickness, I'm going to buy you a bicycle. Al's sunken dark circled eyes lit up like light bulbs. "A bicycle for me?" Responded the surprised boy. "That's what I said," answered the worried father. "Family and friends gave nickels, dimes, and quarters to help pay for the used bike."

Memories like the cigar smoke and the promised bicycle remained with Al throughout his life.

Even though he nearly lost his life in Inglenook, Al loved the town. Speaking of it, he said, "I loved every street and alley. Inglenook was security for me. The town meant friends, love, joy, peace and life itself. Our lives, while living there, were touched with both joy and sadness. I remember my dad losing his job as a printer. It was because of the lack of jobs that my brother, Walter, joined the Navy.

I remember, too, how pop came through with the bicycle when I got well again. We didn't have much money but when pop made a promise, there was no question about him keeping it. When he brought the bicycle home with him, I couldn't believe how beautiful it looked. Pop and mama had big smiles on their faces as they watched me admire that most wonderful gift. It was the most beautiful thing I ever saw," said Al. "I could hardly believe that it was mine."

There wasn't any doubt in Al's mind that God existed and He was to be revered as being great and good. "I remember lying in bed at night with my teeth hurting and asking Jesus to please take the pain away. My parents did not have money to take me to a dentist."

Al recalls that in his early days of school, they did not play baseball, softball or football at recess time. "Our basketball hoops were always broken and I don't ever remember seeing a net. Underneath each broken, net-less hoop was usually a pool of water or mud. It did not matter if the ground was wet or dry because none of us had a basketball which we could use to play."

Things changed greatly when Al's father took over as director of the summer program. "We had a great time in the summer when my daddy was the director. He loved baseball and wanted each kid to perform his best.

One thing we did play a lot of was marbles. That was a lot of fun. We played for keeps. That meant if any one won my marbles they kept them. The same was true if I won marbles from one of my friends. I don't know why, but I turned out to be the champion marble player of our school. Another game we played a lot was horseshoes. I know we actually didn't do it, but now as I look back, it seemed like we played horse shoes all day long at times." When asked when he first started playing baseball, Al said "It wasn't until I was ten yeas old that I played on my first organized baseball team. Our mother made our uniforms. We were called the Red Birds. Inglenook seemed to have a baseball team for every age group. I started out playing third base but after a few balls hit me on my shins I told the manager that I really was a pitcher because I could throw strikes. I don't remember much more about that first organized team that I played on but one of the things I do remember was how good it felt to hit the ball. I remember, too, that I learned to throw a curve and was able to strike out the batters.

Another thing that I remember during those days as I became bigger and stronger were the football games we played. We really played tough football. It was not the easy touch football that I have seen some play but rather the rough tackle football. As I look back now, I smile as I think of the danger we were putting ourselves in of being bodily injured. There wasn't much equipment to be seen among the players. In fact, I played half back and ran the ball without a helmet. Our opposing teams came from nearby communities. Now and then there would be a brawl, which would end the game."

The town of Inglenook was an exciting place to be during the Christmas holidays. Al described it as, "The most fun place on earth." He went on to say, "For two weeks we skated in front of Inglenook school. We blocked the street off from all traffic except skates. Old and young alike skated long into the night. The two weeks that we were out of school flew by too fast."

Al's eyes seemed to flicker with excitement as he spoke about events of his youth. "I remember one time when my fifth grade teacher, Mrs. Alexander, called me outside the classroom. When I got outside the door, there stood a woman with a sweater for me to try on. I was so embarrassed that I stuck my arm way up into the sweater to make it look like it didn't fit. I really did not want them to give me a sweater. When it got cold enough I would wear both my sweaters. I did have two sweaters but both were filled with holes. I wore both of them at the same time so the top sweater would cover the holes in the one underneath.

One of the things that I did which I am not proud of was to steal peaches from our next-door neighbor. I took a long pole and tied a tin can on the end of it. I would then reach over the fence with the pole, put the can underneath a peach, flip the peach into the can, pull the can back, and enjoy eating the peach.

It is amazing," said Al, "how I could steal at that time and think it was so funny. Stealing seemed to be a part of life." Even at his young age, Al did some things for which he is not proud. He said, "I smoked my first cigarette in the fourth grade. A grocery store down the street sold cigarettes to the kids for a penny a piece. Thoughts of those bad things which I did seem to remain clear in my memory."

Al was twelve years old when Japan attacked Pearl Harbor on December 7, 1941. He was a paperboy at the time. "I remember yelling as loud as I could, "Extra, extra, war with Japan." The people came out of their houses to buy a paper from me for five cents. The days, months, and years to follow saw many changes. Two things that I recall rationed were gasoline and sugar. There were eleven of us at home at the time. Each one of us had a jar with our name on it.

We each used the sugar from our own individual jar. Of course, if someone ran out of sugar, one of us would share our sugar with him or her. As far as gasoline was concerned, that was not a problem to us because we did not own a car."

During part of the war years, the Worthington family put baseball on hold. Speaking of the love of the family for baseball and softball, Al said, "The ball diamond was a family place for my bothers and sisters. That's right," he emphasized, "All of my sisters played softball and they were good at it. Looking back on our family's activities, baseball and softball would be at the top of the list.

We did not play baseball for some three years," said Al, "Most of the boys had gone to war."

As Al reflected on his past, he thought of how he earned money by cutting grass. "I cut grass, for twenty-five cents a lawn during the summer. There was a time that the grass was so high I could not push the lawn mower through it. I called my brother Oliver to help me. I got a sickle and cut it close to the ground and then we ran the mower over it."

Al loved grammar school. In fact, he said it was the best time of schooling in his life. Thinking of going to high school scared him even though he was one of the bigger boys in the school. "Phillips High School seemed so big to me," Al remarked. "The enormous size of the building scared me. It sat on the space of a town block and it was three stories high. I remember that I started high school in January 1944.

Even though I was in high school, I still thought of my grammar school days. I had a paper route, worked at Tidwell Drug Store for ten cents an hour, and also ushered at the Alabama Theater. My friends, Cotton Crawford, George Burris, and J. O. Richards were very much a part of my life. I got into the habit of smoking with them and it was a bad habit that I did not quit until many years later."

First and only baby picture

Grammar school days

Al at fifteen

We thumbed to Miami

High School Track
Team 1946

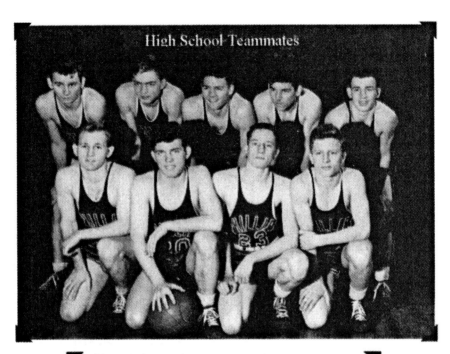

High School Teammates

Running Track

Phillips Baseball Teammates

High School Freshman

High School Basketball

Number 11

Facing a World of Opportunity

4

MEMORIES - GOOD
AND BAD

Al was never far in thought from his earlier school years. With the school not a great distance away, he always walked to and from school. "Those days were something else," Al said grinning. "We kept busy alright but our business was throwing rocks at telephone poles. Perhaps all that throwing helped to develop my pitching arm.

Our family did not own an automobile so riding was not an option. I did a lot of things during my elementary school days but the thing that stands out the most in my memory was that my mother would be home when I got there. Not realizing it at the time, my dear mother made a life time impression on me because of the way she gave herself unselfishly and without reservation for her children."

Once Al started talking about his boyhood days, there was no stopping him. His eyes lit up when telling stories of his younger days. It was like he was living the events all over again. "The State Fair came to town, but I did not have money to go," he said with his boyish smile, "I had a nickel and I spent it on a bag of peanuts. You would not believe the size of that bag of peanuts for only a nickel. It was filled to the top. I headed for the schoolyard. Upon arriving there, I found a nice quiet spot where I sat down and enjoyed eating every peanut. One time, my friend Cotton, paid my way to the fair and even got me a date. On that special occasion, Cotton and I treated our dates by riding the streetcar.

Usually every group of kids has a favorite place to sit and talk. Our special place was on the street curb. We did this night after night during the summer months. I mentioned previously that I started smoking at a young age. I was actually nine-years old. Only once do I remember having a whole pack of cigarettes to myself. I usually bummed what I smoked from Cotton. He always had cigarettes. I never took them into our house. There was a place in the bushes outside where I hid them. It would not have gone well with me at all if my daddy had caught me with them."

Another thing that stood out in Al's memory was the fifty cents that his sister, Evelynn, gave him each week. "She worked as a waitress and earned $25.00 a week."

Money was scarce and hard to come by at the Worthington household. Pop and mama dearly loved their children and tried to do special things for them in spite of funds being scarce. "We could always count on eating watermelon on the fourth of July," Al recalled. "I can still see my daddy walking home from the store with two watermelons under his arms. I don't know how he did it as he walked for at least a half-mile. We really enjoyed eating watermelon as a fourth of July special. Another weekly treat was on Friday nights when pop paid the grocery bill. For paying the bill he was given a bag of jellybeans. It seems like I can taste them now. It really did not take much to make us children happy.

In the Hale Avenue house where I was sick, we did not have an electric refrigerator but rather an icebox. Mama had a square card about ten inches across. It had the numbers of 20, 40, 50 and 60 on it. All that mama had to do was hang the card in the window with the number of pounds of ice she wanted. The iceman would stop his truck, read the number on top, take his pick and cut the block of ice mama needed. He then would put the ice in the icebox and we would be fixed for several more days. The icebox was a big help to mama who had to keep certain foods cool."

Another thing that Al did which he is not proud of was to start gambling. At the age of thirteen, he took a job pedaling papers. The paperboys would gather at the paper branch house. Someone would draw a line in the sand or dirt. The boys then would line up a certain distance and toss quarters toward the line to see who came the nearest. Al said that he liked picking up his winnings.

Al was exceptionally talented in sports. At Phillips High School he played four sports. He said, "I had never seen a basketball game until I went to high school. Probably another thing difficult to understand is that baseball was my worst sport in high school. I have been told that high school years were the best years of a person's life. I did not think that back then and I don't think it now. I must confess, however, they were not bad years. I disliked playing football even though I was not a bad football player.

In order to play sports well, it takes lots of practice and practice was always after school let out for the day. For four years I hitchhiked to and from school. A few times I rode the streetcar but like I said, hitchhiking was usually the way I traveled back and forth. I always came home late. I would get out at 37th Avenue and walk home in the dark. Many times, there wasn't anything to eat which made my mama feel terrible. In a way, it was to my advantage that the supper food was gone because then I could ask mama to fix a pot of beans for me. I can still hear myself saying, "Mama, put me on a pot of beans and I'll be happy." She would do that and I ate like a king. I would sit there and eat every bean and thought I was the luckiest fellow in the world."

Going to high school was not a problem for Al. The problem for him was getting out of bed in the morning. Al said, "The hardest thing about going to high school was getting up. My mama got me up. They would not stand for any disrespect from us children. I remember one day when we were gathered at the table, Oliver, who was seventeen, said something to mama that was not nice. My father, who was not at the table when we all sat down, walked into the room and heard what Oliver said to mama. Without saying a word, pop walked over to Oliver and hit him on the side of his face. Oliver flew off his chair and ended up under the kitchen sink. We all learned a good lesson that day-to love and respect our parents even more than we did before pop hit Oliver.

As I said, mama got me up so I wouldn't be late for school. I usually made my own breakfast. The frying pan already had the grease in it so all I had to do was drop in the eggs. Mama made biscuits each morning so with fresh biscuits, two eggs and rice, I had a delicious breakfast fit for a king.

Mama stopped making biscuits during my sixteenth year. She decided to make toast instead. For a sixteen year old who was used to eating biscuits in the morning, bread is a long way from eating mama's biscuits. I loved to make sandwiches with biscuits and tomatoes. I loved eating tomatoes back then, but somehow over the years, I lost my taste for them.

Another thing, which I remember well, was how daddy always prayed before our meals. We kids knew what he was going to say because it was the same repetitive prayer. There were times we would start laughing. Mama would sometimes join us. Pop never cracked a smile nor did he say anything.

Even though I never doubted the existence of God and even prayed, I really did not know Him as my heavenly Father. During my high school years, I thought a lot about God. I had the gut feeling that there was something very important missing from my life.

In fact, from the time I had pneumonia, I never lost the desire of thinking about God. Even when I was doing wrong things, I still never doubted the fact that God knew all about me. I prayed each night since that terrible illness that nearly took my life. My prayers were usually repetition prayers. God was in my thoughts, but spiritually, He was far away. I wanted to get closer to Him but did not know how to do it nor did I know of anyone who could tell me how to do it; not even our pastor.

I prayed a lot when I was young. I knew I wanted to go to heaven when I died but I really didn't know what I should do to go there. As far as I can remember, I always believed in God. If any one would ask me if I loved God, I would be quick to tell them that I did. Like many people in this world, I was not an enemy to God. I just did not know Him as my Heavenly Father."

When asked about his childhood years and even into his years at Phillips High School, Al said, "It really did not seem to me that we were poor. Many of my friends were in the same boat. If I had to live my life over again, I don't think that I could have it any better. I had wonderful parents who loved me and cared for me. I had good brothers and sisters who loved me. There was a roof over my head, I had clothes to wear and there was always food to eat. I can't think of anything more wonderful than having all that."

5

SPORT CHALLENGES AT PHILLIPS HIGH

Teenage Al Worthington wanted to play as many sports in high school as he possibly could even though he wasn't keen on baseball. Al was a big boy weighing 156 pounds his first year at Phillips High School. It was a large school drawing students from all over the city of Birmingham. With a large student body, there were many from which to choose for the sports teams. "It was a squad of big players," Al said. "Training began in March for the football team. The first day of practice, I came out on the field in my Sunday shoes. I only had one pair of shoes to wear and they were not football shoes. I was the only one out for practice wearing street shoes but as strange as it sounds, it did not matter at all to me. I knew in my heart that I would make the team and play football for Phillips. I felt that way even before I went to Phillips High School. A few days after practice started, the equipment manager gave me a pair of football shoes.

"I didn't know the fundamentals of the game. I could catch the football and I was a good punter. I dreaded what I called head on tackles. The drill required two lines of players facing each other about ten yards apart. When the whistle blew, the players would try and tackle the one opposite of him, it was a terrible drill for me."

Sandy haired Al looked forward so much to playing for the Red Raiders of Phillips High and at last he had his chance. Coach Red Houston was open with his thoughts about his 1946 Raiders. After all, he had only 13 lettermen from the season before. He told the press that his boys needed a lot of work before they would be winning many games. Al got the starting position at left end about the fourth game. Team Captain Norman "Fatty" Box and the rest of the squad were confident they could take on and give every team in their schedule a battle.

Al was nervous but anxious as the Raiders took the field against Walker County High School of Jasper. It was a hard fought battle against the Vikings before a screaming crowd of 7,500 people at Legion Field. Al's nervousness quickly vanished once the game started. The deciding play of the game took place from the Walker 25 yard line when number 55, Billy Branch, threw a pass to Al who caught it and ran into the end zone for the touchdown. The extra point conversion attempt was blocked and that is the way the game ended. Their first game of the 1946 season was won 6 - 0. The season gave Al the opportunity to develop and show his skills. A local sports writer described Al as one of the finest prep school punters we have ever seen. A beautiful description by a writer covering the high school teams said that Al was by far the town's most outstanding punter. He went on to say that Al's talented toe ranked second only to his glue-covered fingers.

Phillips win over the Woodlawn Colonels that football season was another hard fought game. Al led the Phillips Red Raiders to victory with his outstanding punting keeping the opposing Woodlawn squad back in their own territory. The Colonels hit pay dirt once when the team captain Billy Hallmark, stepped in the way of a pass and with the intercepted ball, ran from three yards behind the goal line, 103 yards for a Woodlawn touchdown. Al's punting average for the game was 39.3.

The Phillips High School football star, even though heaped with praise from teachers and students, alike, did not forget his beloved parents or brothers and sisters, who were proud of him. The newspapers in the area were consistent in carrying pictures and articles about the football star. A writer telling of Al's performance said that it was out of this world. He was confident that he could catch and punt with the best on the high school level.

At sixteen years old and a high school junior, Al was getting bigger and stronger. Number 11 started the season at 174 pounds. Even though he was a better than average football player and a star in the minds of many of the students and town people, Al did not entirely like the game. Years later, he said, "Football practice was a dreaded thing. I really hated practice. The games were fun but not fun enough to spend all that time practicing. Everyday I prayed for rain so we would not have to practice. The trouble was, playing football was not like playing baseball. It can rain and the football game or even practice goes on. It would take a very hard rainstorm to stop a football game. Rain can stop a baseball game quite easily. When that baseball gets wet, it can do some crazy things on its way to the plate."

In talking about his football days at Phillips High School, Al admitted that his favorite place was not making a difficult catch of a pass thrown to him or even picking his way through the opposing players for a touchdown. He said, "I loved the school shower. I remember after a game going into the shower and bathing, in that nice warm water. We did not have a shower at home so I enjoyed the one at school as much as possible."

He also recalled how his financial situation improved when he started high school. "When I started high school," Al said, "my Dad gave me $5.00 a week. I knew that I was in the big time. The fifty cents that my sister, Evelynn gave me during my grammar school days was just as precious to me. I love her for the wonderful way she treated me. I can't say enough things about my parents and brothers and sisters. We all were very close to each other."

Playing football for the Phillips High Red Raiders actually was a tremendous privilege for Al as well as a challenge. In his junior year, he was the only player from Phillips chosen for the 1946 all-state team as well as the post all-city team. In fact, Al was the overwhelming choice for one of the end positions. The local paper praised the pride and joy of Coach Red Houston. The newspaper pointed out that Al was one of the finest prep punters ever seen on a local gridiron. It told how Al was very adept at snagging passes and also that he was a deadly tackler. One of the tributes paid to the all-city football team was an invitation to be the guests of the Monday Morning Quarterback Club at the Tutwiler Hotel. Al was honored with a reward for his outstanding playing performance.

Like icing on the cake, Al was selected for one of the end positions of the 1946 all-city team.

At the annual banquet honoring the Phillips High School football squad at McCoy Memorial Church, Allan Fulton Worthington was named Phillips "most valuable man" for his play contributions to the team. What made the honor so great was that he was chosen by his teammates for the honor. "All the fellows deserve this honor," said Al. "Every man on the Phillips' squad worked and played hard this season."

Another high point in the recognition event was when the announcement was made that Allan Worthington was elected to be the team's captain for the 1947 season. "This is unbelievable," thought Al. "For my first appearance to try out for the team, I wore street shoes because I didn't even have football shoes. Now here I am being elected to be the captain of the team."

"Everybody is trying. Everybody is working." Said Coach 'Shot' Senn in his first public appraisal of his new team. The new coach from Auburn where he was an assistant was encouraged with the great talent of his all-state end, Al Worthington. For the 1947 season, Al would play double duty again. When the situation called for a punt, Al would move into the backfield. During his senior football season, Captain Al gave it everything he had. He received his letter and caught the attention of a number of colleges and universities but there was an unfortunate ending for the 1947 season for Al. He said years later, "Toward the end of the schedule, I turned my ankle and missed about four games so that was the season for me."

Making the basketball team at Phillips High was another challenge for Al. "I had the height," said Al, "so if I could dribble the ball and hit the basket, I figured I had as good a chance as any of the others trying out for the team. Coach Ernest Tucker liked what he saw in Al and when the basketball season started, Allan Fulton Worthington was playing the starting center position. Playing all home games in the Municipal Auditorium was welcome news for players and fans alike. It could seat a lot of people and the admission had to be a bargain at twenty-five cents.

In basketball as it was in football, the sports writers praised the all-around sports star. One writer wrote, "Worthington, a snazzy pass snatcher from the gridiron is, to the opinion of many, the most promising center Phillips has had in many years." The Phillips Red Raiders showed an example of their court strength when they won over the Hewitt Quintet by the score of 66-22. Al shot five baskets and had two free throws for a total of 12 points. The "B" team referred to, as the "Little Red Streaks" were victors in a lopsided game that they won 60-9. It was the second game of the season for the Raiders.

One of the strongest games probably ever played at home by Phillips was against the State champions from Selma. The strategy used by the Red Raiders was to freeze the ball and keep the state champs from scoring. The unbelievable final score was Selma 8 and Phillips 4. In the first half alone, the Red Raiders froze the ball for 14 minutes and 50 seconds.

The local sports writers were all but making wagers with each other that Phillips' star center would not be able to play in the Ensley game because of an eye injury received in a game with West End the week before. "My eye hurt," said the star center, "but I was determined to get into the game if at all possible." Coach Tucker sent Al to see a doctor hoping that something could be done to help him. Al did play that afternoon at the auditorium and surprised everyone present, except himself, in racking up 17 of the 52 winning points. It came time for the choosing of the first and second teams of the Post's "all-Big Five" quintet. The five schools made the selection. Al barely lost to the star center of the Woodlawn Colonels.

Being the good sportsman he was, the man with 24 on his jersey was happy for the player chosen over him for the first team. Al stood tall and proud with his teammates for the Phillips' basketball team picture.

"I remember one time when Coach Tucker told me that I shot too much," said Al with that familiar smile on his face, "He also told the other players to shoot more. I didn't mind him saying that because he knew what he was talking about and he really did want to see me do my best but as a team player. I especially liked Coach Tucker and I greatly respected him as a coach and as a gentleman. I may not have enjoyed his discipline back then but the principle of it stuck with me. He blistered many boys with his paddle. I remember the time when Coach caught me shooting the basketball on the gym floor with my street shoes on. That was definitely a no-no back then as well as it is today. I deserved the punishment. Another time he saw me standing up in gym class when I was supposed to be seated. As I look back on those days under Coach Tucker, I see him so many times as an example for me. He was a solid guy. He did not smoke or swear. I regret so much that I did those things. I suppose I could have been worse than I was had it not been for Coach Tucker.

It was a memorable evening when Coach Tucker commended our teams for our success. My last basketball game, I felt so good when he handed me my varsity letter for basketball."

Being such an all around athlete, Al went out for the track and field team at Phillips High. "This sure isn't anything like football or even basketball," Al remarked to one of his teammates one day at practice, "but I'm going to give it all I have." The strapping 175-pounder decided to do the shot put. In his mind, big Al thought he could throw the heavy ball as far as he needed to throw it to win over his opponents.

"I don't recall very much about my performances in high school," said Al when asked about the track meets in which he participated. "I remember the time we defeated Bessemer. It was our first victory of the season. Jimmy Walker and I were the top point makers for Phillips. I made thirteen points and Jimmy made eleven and one-fourth points. That was some meet. I placed third in the high hurdles. I was always fearful that my feet would knock them over which they did many times. I must have been eating my spinach because in the shot put competition, I threw that ball 103 feet and took first place. That was some throw. When the ball left my hand, it just seemed to take off like it had wings on it. I couldn't believe my own eyes. For the high jump that day, I came in second. Even 5 feet 6 inches is a long way up there for my 175 pounds to clear the cross bar. I felt pretty good with my broad jump when my feet left the ground and didn't touch again until I had traveled 18 feet 6 inches. On that jump, I tied for first place with a fellow by the name of Willoughby."

Speaking about the Alabama High School Track Meet one year, Al described his own amazement of his accomplishments. He said, "I qualified on Friday for the finals on Saturday. On Friday, I was leading in the shot put competition. It was a cold day at Legion Field. Bill Curley, who had won the high hurdles and low hurdles at Phillips, as well as the low hurdles at Auburn, rubbed my legs with something right before the high hurdles run. I left him and got into position. I believe there were eight or ten of us for that final run and we represented the best in the entire State of Alabama. I kept asking myself how did I make it to be part of such an illustrious group of runners. The gun went off and as I glided over the first hurdle, I looked back and the others were just starting to move. One thing I did well was to get a good start. I usually was off with the crack of the gun. I kept telling myself that I could win the race. I ran as fast as my legs would take me. I remember knocking down seven hurdles in that race. I ended up finishing third in the entire State of Alabama. As I recall, a new high school record was set for the high hurdles in that race. The thing that really surprised me was that I didn't look upon myself as a high hurdles runner. When I was given my letter for track and field, it made me feel good that I had accomplished something for Phillips High, myself, and my family who were 100% for me."

When Al committed himself to playing in a sport, he didn't know what it was to not give his all. When he played football for the Crimson Raiders, giving his best was not an option. The same was true for basketball and track and field. The name, Allan Worthington, was the topic of countless conversations not only in the Birmingham area but also throughout the State of Alabama.

6

HELP IN MAKING THE RIGHT DECISION

"I know this sounds strange," said Al laughing, "but I didn't like football when I went to Phillips. In fact, I even quit the football team. When I played, I played hard but I didn't like it like basketball and track and field and even baseball. When my brother heard that I quit, he really got onto me. He told me that I would be the quitter in the Worthington family. My dad was even more upset when he heard that I had quit the team. He told me that I was yellow. The meaning of yellow to me was that I was afraid and couldn't take the pressure. When dad told me that, and Oliver said I would be the only quitter in our family, I went back and told the coach I was ready to play.

Once I got back into it, I really enjoyed playing football for Phillips High. I was ashamed of myself. I'm glad for what my dad and my brother, Oliver, said to me. It was a good lesson I had to learn. As I look back on my life, it was an extremely important lesson that had a major effect on my future and me. Our family loved each other. When I think of pop saying that I was yellow, I knew he said it in love and for my best. The same is true of what Oliver said about me being the first quitter in our family. He wanted me to be ashamed of what I was doing and he was very successful in his first attempt.

Don't think that it was easy for me to go face Coach Houston. Like I said, I went back and told him that I was ready to play. I don't know what I would have done had he said no to me because of what I did. I do know one thing for sure; pop would have been up to the school as quick as lightening. I'm glad it turned out the way it did. I made the right decision even if I did have some pretty good help from pop and Oliver.

I believe I played with some of the finest players on the high school level. Every year I played in high school was enjoyable and there were many high points that I remember. I especially recall making the East-West All-Star Baseball Team in my junior year. I know that one of the biggest encouragements to me was my dad and mother. Not one time did either of them criticize me or belittle me. I received only words of encouragement and slaps on the back."

The East-West All-Star Game was the game of the year. It pitted against each other some of the very best high school players. Al has in one of his numerous scrapbooks of his exciting life, a Certificate of Merit dating back to 1946. It reads, "Champions All, Certificate of Merit. This Certificate of Merit is awarded to Allan Worthington a member of the East-West Baseball game, for his unselfish efforts in raising funds for the Alabama Sight Conservation Association, Inc. For the East-West Game played in 1946. L. W. Hurt, Secretary, Alabama Sight Conservation Assn., Inc."

The newspaper carried a picture of Al with Loy Vaughn, one of the West's coaching staff, holding the certificate described above. Al said, "There were 32 of us who were presented with a certificate for being selected to play in the East-West Game on the night of June 28, 1946. I was honored to be a member of the East team and to be a guest of the downtown Lion's Club at their luncheon at the Thomas Jefferson Hotel."

Red Houston, who coached the Phillips baseball team, was chosen to be the coach of the East Team. When Coach Houston presented Al with his letter in baseball at the close of the regular high school season, Al joined Ben Chapman and Fred Sington on the Phillips four-letter honor roll.

Looking back on the East-West game in 1946 that was played at Rickwood Field, Al said, "I just appreciated being in the game that day. I pitched in the seventh inning and to tell the truth, I didn't pitch well. Coach Houston pulled out Byron Mathews who had loaded the bases and put me in to pitch to Clifford Reach. I walked Reach and Jack Maxwell in succession forcing in two runs. Dick Morgan then lined a single to center field scoring two more runs. Tom Smith of Woodlawn High School then relieved me and I was put in right field. I knew if a ball was hit to me, I would not have been surprised if it hit me on the head. When I was on the mound and looked at the people sitting behind the screen, I got scared. I don't remember looking into faces behind the screen like I saw that night. I swung with one hand and struck out. My nervousness paid off but not for me. It was the worst night of my life. I honestly was afraid to go home after the game.

My older brothers, Walter and Oliver who played professional baseball, were at the game. What would they say to me? Would my dad say anything to me? I arrived home at 2:00 a.m. that was the latest I ever stayed out. I wanted everyone to be asleep when I got home. The front screen door was unlocked and I quietly went to my bed. I finally went to sleep thinking about the game and especially the poor showing that I made. I awoke about 9:30 and was glad when I found out that the house was empty except for my mother.

I got up and started moving around the room. Mama came into my room and said, "Allan" she spoke in a whisper, "I thought you did so well last night. Only one player hit the ball." I wondered why mama whispered. I looked at my dear mama and said, "Thank you." I don't think that my mother knew what a walk was and I wasn't about to tell her. She may not have known much about the fundamentals of baseball, but she sure knew how to raise her children. Both mama and pop were a great source of encouragement to me. Mama's words kept running through my mind. "You did well last night."

I'm so glad the game came out the way it did. We played as a team but if there is one player who deserved praise for his contribution for the 10 to 8 win, it was J. C. Powers who hit three doubles, scored twice, and batted in four runs. Our second baseman, Jimmy Bragan, was voted the number two player of the game.   Jimmy's brother, Bobby Bragan played with the Philadelphia Phillies and the Brooklyn Dodgers."

The honored guests attending the East-West game created an atmosphere that matched or surpassed events in major league games. The notables included the High Commissioner of Baseball, A. B. "Happy" Chandler; the president of the Southern Association Baseball League, Billy Evans; network announcer, Mel Allen, who announced for Kate Smith and Kay Kyser and who became famous in the baseball world as the Voice of the New York Yankees.

Thinking of his years at Phillips High School and all the challenges he faced and the thrills he experienced on the gridiron, the baseball diamond, the track and field events, and the basketball court, Al's eyes glistened as a slight smile appeared on his aging face. "I loved Phillips High School when I went there," he said. "Memories are pretty wonderful. But like most every thing in life, you leave it and take the next step in life. For me, my next step was the University of Alabama."

7

NEXT STEP - UNIVERSITY OF ALABAMA

Many scouts watched the promising young men from Phillips High School during each game. Now it was decision time for Al. He said with a grin, "I had to make up my mind. It was either the army or college. The decision was not too difficult at that time. The war was over so I chose college. Mississippi State wanted me to play baseball and basketball for them."

Al's dad was always supportive of him and was there to give advice when asked. "You know your mother and I are behind you," said his dad one day. We're not worried about you making the wrong decision." Al felt the best thing he had going for him was the support of his entire family.

He said, "I visited Auburn University and probably could have gone there, but never officially was offered a scholarship. A scholarship had to be part of the deal because I didn't have the funds to pay my way and I knew my parents didn't have that kind of money. Auburn was 125 miles from Inglenook and if I went there, I would probably not get back home much. With that in mind, I chose the University of Alabama. One thing I did not want to do was to play football in college."

"Before I left for Alabama, my two older brothers and my dad went down town to buy me some clothes. They spent $60.00 on me that day. I don't know if I even owned a pair of underwear or even a pair of socks. I think everything I wore belonged to Oliver. He played professional baseball and was able to buy nice clothes. In high school, I looked pretty good in Oliver's clothes. When he left for spring training with the St. Louis Cardinals farm team and took his clothes with him--that left me with a problem. My source of nice clothes was gone. The following summer, I paid back the $60.00.

I remember the day I left for the University of Alabama. I think I cried all the way to school. It was only 60 miles away but that was like a thousand miles to me. My heart was broken to leave home. I loved my home. Unknown to me, my daddy, who was always looking out for me, told the coach at the University not to put me in a room with anyone who drank. The coach told my dad that they didn't have anyone who drank. My dad, who had been around the block more than once, looked at the coach. The mileage on my dad's face spoke volumes. They put me in a room with a fellow by the name of Jack Rutledge. He was a peach of a man. Jack played shortstop on the baseball team.

Jack discovered my weaknesses immediately. One was that I didn't want to go to any of my classes. He tried to help me but I just would not listen to him. As I look back on it now, I see how dumb and unwise I was at the time. I am embarrassed now to even think of how I was so foolish. I only remember one class and that was a class on government. As the professor talked, the students took notes. That was all new to me. I don't really recall taking notes in high school. To tell you the truth, I was lost. I had no idea what was going on in class. After a week or so, I found out that I could drop a class. I did just that."

Al was beginning to see himself as he actually was. Could it be possible that his talents in sports brought him to where he was? He said, "In high school, I never studied and my bad grades proved that. It seems that I entered high school and left four years later without opening a book. When I got to Alabama, I really did not know how to study. Again, I say all of this to my shame. One of the things that I enjoyed at the University was the good food. I ate very well. Life at school was all right but I just did not seem to fit in there.

When the baseball season started, because I was a freshman, I played for the freshman team. I remember that we played three games. Every chance I got to go back home, I did. I was dissatisfied with school and I loved my home and wanted to be there. That was a bad combination for one who is supposed to be in college.

Things began to open up for me a bit when the baseball season ended. Jack Rutledge and another player got me a pitching job at Metter, Georgia, for $400.00 a month. To me, that was better than hauling dirt or working in a factory. Talking by phone with the baseball man at Metter one night he said, "I want you to come here as soon as you can. Come by plane." I told the man that to go by plane cost a lot of money. I heard him slap his wallet. He said, "I have lots of money back here. I want you here in Metter."

I went to Metter. It was a very small town and very hot at the time. Several of us lived in one room at a woman's house. It was a large room for which we were thankful. It seems like all I did there was smoke, pitch ball and sit around on the curb down town and eat watermelon that we stole from the nearby fields.

I'll never forget a trip we made one time from Metter to Jessup, Georgia. We went by car and I must confess, we traveled somewhat over the speed limit. All of us were enjoying the ride when all of a sudden, one of the guys yelled, "What's that in the

47

road up ahead?" "Those are cows, you dummy," answered someone in the back seat. "Don't you know a cow when you see it?" Laughing about the trip, Al said, "Those cows acted just like they owned the road. I know one thing for sure," he continued, "there must be laws now in Georgia for cows!"

Al began to develop arm trouble at Metter. When he pitched, his elbow would begin to hurt around the fourth or fifth inning. When he threw the curve ball, he would snap his elbow. The fastball didn't cause him any trouble. After pitching a game, he could not straighten out his arm the next morning. It took about four days for his arm to feel good enough for him to pitch again. The baseball season came to a close and it was time for football at the University of Alabama. He knew he would miss that $400.00 a month playing baseball.

"I was not physically ready for the football season," said Al. "I should have been running every day. Practice began that year of 1948 on September 1. It was so hot, I could hardly move at times. We had two practices a day. The one in the morning, we wore shorts. That felt pretty good. After practice was over in the morning, I always went and got something to eat and then went to my room to rest. You can be sure; I rested as much as I could. We wore our pads for the afternoon practice. The coach had us cross our legs each time we took a step for a distance of ten yards. I wasn't in any shape for that kind of punishment. I felt that if I had to go back the ten yards I would have died. I never put a strain on my body like that before. The whistle blew and head coach Red Drew, called all of us together at the end of the field where the bleachers were located. I felt like I was going to drop any moment. High School football practice was never that hard.

I climbed to the top row and lay down. There was a wonderful breeze blowing. For years I believed that the breeze actually kept me from passing out. We all were sprawled out on the bleachers enjoying the rest. For the rest of the season, Coach Drew did not call for a meeting by the bleachers."

Could Al come anywhere near to what he did playing for Phillips High? The 18 year old received good press. Even before the season opened, one writer had him already teamed up in a pass combination with Eddie Salem, a former all-southern player at

Ramsay High School. The two former opponents would have the opportunity of uniting their talents for Alabama. In practice sessions, Al was beginning to get a lot of respect from the Crimson Tide backs as he played defense. More than one sports writer referred to Al as one of the greatest kickers in Birmingham prep history. They also rated him as a top pass receiver. Now he was getting the opportunity to show his ability on the college level. Not all the press was encouraging for Al. One writer wrote that Alabama was stocked with ends and that young Al would have to be very good in order to see a lot of action.

Speaking of football at Alabama, Al said, "Like I said before I didn't go to very many classes. I took just enough hours to be eligible for football. I did not like it at Alabama and I admit that I was not a good student. I was not a good example for anyone and I am so sorry about that. There are areas of my life that I wish I could live over again knowing what I know now. I suppose most people feel like that."

8

INJURIES-OPERATION-
DETERMINATION

"It was my second year, 1949, when I hurt my left arm in practice. I remember it was one of those morning practice sessions when it happened. We were in shorts because of the heat. It was during a dummy drill when one of the players hit me under my left arm when I was totally relaxed. The impact knocked my left shoulder out of joint. That was the first time that happened to me but it turned out to be that it wasn't the last time. In fact, it came out numerous times after that but I'm thankful that it always went back into place without help.

Being the type of person I am, I felt terrible. I have never been one for loafing or goofing off. I can honestly say that I have always given my best in sports. I finally had a brace put on my arm. To hold my arm up a bit, there was a small chain fastened to it. When I went out for a pass, I would unfasten the chain. This gave me freedom with my arm, especially my left arm. It was my second football season and I didn't play very much. I really did not think that I was fast enough to be the player I wanted to be. Injuries actually ended my football playing for Alabama.

I recall one time in practice, I went out for a short pass. I ran out about ten yards and turned my body to face the passer. The ball was to me but over my head. I jumped as high as I could with my arms stretched above me. At that moment, a player hit me hard in my back. On my way down, someone else hit me. It was the worst pain that I ever had playing football. Coach Laney came over to where I was laying on the ground and said, "Get up Al, you aren't hurt." If he only had known how much I was hurting, I'm sure he would not have said what he did. I got up and forced myself to keep going as coach told me to do. Many years later in 1968, I found out I had a degenerate disc in my back. The doctor said, "You took a very hard hit sometime in the past, Al. Can you recall any accident that you may have had" How could I ever forget that double hit that I took in practice? I knew exactly when it happened. Those two seconds on the field that day have given me some pain every day since."

Al's left shoulder was so bad it affected his playing ability. Something had to be done. In speaking of the 1949 baseball season, Al said, "I batted with one arm. I took my left hand off the bat when I swung at a pitch. It really hurt if I missed hitting the ball. If I kept my left arm on the bat and missed hitting the ball my arm would snap out of joint. If I hit the ball it worked all right.

In December 1949, surgery was done on my left shoulder. When I came out of the anesthesia as they rolled me into my room, I really don't know why I did it but I began to kick and swing my right arm. I was out of control so the attendant lit the emergency light outside my room and called for help. My wonderful mother, who was out in the hall saw the light. She walked into the room and said in her commanding sweet voice, "Allan, you stop right now. You lay down and behave yourself!" I said, "Yes, Mama." That was all it took. An attendant said to me, "When your mother spoke, you knew it was all over." I felt embarrassed later but I still must have been a little bit under the anesthesia. All I can say is that my respect and obedience was so great toward my mother that it cut right through the anesthesia and I heard her loud and clear. When I finally came out of it, I saw that my left arm was taped to my stomach. Little did I realize then that my left arm was going to remain in that position for six weeks. Playing football took a real toll on my body."

"How's the shoulder, Al?" asked one of his friends who knew Al wanted to continue pitching baseball for Alabama. "It hurts when I move my arm," answered Al, "but I'm going to give it my best shot."

Al found it nearly impossible to raise his left arm. When the catcher returned the ball to him, it was difficult for him to stretch for it. The tall college student was determined to overcome the painful handicap and play his best. The more he exercised the arm, the stronger it became and the better he felt. He still had to swing the bat with only his right arm but he found that he not only could hit the ball but he could do it with power.

Al remembers the opening game of the 1950 baseball season. Alabama's Crimson Tide played Stetson University on March 20. Stetson scored all their three runs in the second inning. The heart breaker is that none of their runs were earned. Frank Lary and Al, who came in to pitch the last six innings, held the Florida team to a total of two hits. Alabama lost to Stetson 3 – 2.

Another heart breaker was played on April 12. In a game with Louisiana State University, Al pitched hitless ball through seven and one third innings. He lost his two-hitter 4 – 0.

The Alabama baseball season saw a very much-improved Al Worthington.

The Crimson Tide won the Southeastern Conference baseball championship in 1950. Coach Tilden "Happy" Campbell felt pretty good with the accomplishments of his team and saw no reason why they would not do well again in 1951.

Al tells how close he came to not playing for Alabama. He said, "Billy Hildebrand tried to recruit me for Mississippi State University and he almost had me. I was trying to get a baseball scholarship. Finally it was play football or not to attend school at all. I could not afford it otherwise so I went to Alabama."

Speaking of Al's football ability, Billy Hildebrand said, "Worthington was one of the top ends in our league." Coach Happy Campbell, who was a scout for the Boston Red Sox, commented one day that Frank Lary and Al Worthington were two young players with a chance to make the big leagues. The Detroit Tigers eventually signed Frank. Al thought a lot of Frank Lary and admired his pitching ability. Years later in speaking of Frank, he said, "Frank was a tough pitcher. One year he beat the New York Yankees seven times. He became known as the 'Yankee Killer'." He already mentioned that Sal Maglie of the New York Giants was known as the "Dodger Killer." Al was in his junior year and he, along with his teammates, wanted to take the SEC (Southeastern Conference) and go to Omaha, Nebraska, to play in the College World Series. Having won four without a loss the year before, Al had gained confidence in his pitching.

As much as Allan Worthington tried to swing the bat with two hands on it, he just could not do it. In the game against Mississippi State, Al showed his power at the plate swinging from the right side with one hand. In the game he had two hits, a single and a double. Al, with number 18 on the back of his uniform, led his team in beating Mississippi State by 11 to 5 while clinching what was called the Loop Baseball Title. For the game, he had five at bats, got two hits, scored one run, and struck out three.

With Al and Frank Lary being the core of Bama's pitching staff, the Tide had another good season defeating Auburn 5 - 4, Louisiana State 5 – 4, Mississippi State 10 – 1, Stetson 10 – 5 to name some.

Al's performance in his years of baseball for Bama's Crimson Tide was an eye catching 12 wins against 2 losses. When asked about his pitching for Alabama, he said, "I believe I did pretty good for Coach Campbell. Nine of my 12 victories came during my last two years. I had 4 - 0 and 5 – 0 those years." Even though the big right-hander had a 9 – 0 record his last two years for Alabama, he had the scouts shaking their heads in confusion. The general feeling among them was that they wanted to offer him a contract but they were afraid to take that risk because of the arm and shoulder trouble he had experienced.

Al said, "We finally clinched the Southeastern Conference Title by winning over the University of Kentucky 9 – 1. After winning that title, we went to Concord, North Carolina, to play Clemson and Wake Forest, the best in the conference. We had to win that tournament to qualify for Omaha and the College World Series. Kentucky was the other team from the SEC. We won and went to Omaha.

It was the month of June and we traveled by train. I won't forget that trip because of the experience I had with a chicken dinner that I ordered. It cost $3. When it came, I was disappointed as I looked at the piece of chicken, there was no meat to speak of. It seemed I was hungrier when I finished then when I started. It was some 12 years before I got up enough courage to order chicken again."

The team arrived and was happy to the man that the trip by train was ended. Frank Lary was chosen by Coach Happy Campbell to pitch the first game.

"We were all excited to be in the College World Series," said the Fulton Spring player. "Frank Lary started the first game against Bradley University. We won the game. I was not too fortunate with the game I started. It was against Washington State. We lost which eliminated us from the tournament. Needless to say, it was a tremendous disappointment to us. I believe a major factor in our sub performance was the weather. We had a good team; in fact, I believe we had a team, which could have won the series. The weather was cold and there was a lot of fog. To really describe the weather situation, the fog was so thick at times; the outfielder could not locate the balls hit to them. Like I said, we were disappointed but not ashamed of our playing."

9

FULDA - WHERE MY DREAMS CAME TRUE

There to look at the talent of the players were two men from Fulda, Minnesota, they approached Frank Lary about playing semi-pro ball in Minnesota for the summer. He told the men to talk with Al. They wasted no time in going to Al.

"It was not a bad deal they offered me," said Al. "They told me they would pay me $500 a month to pitch for their local team in the First Night League. The man who made the offer was Dick Reusse. There was no way for me to return home to Alabama to see my family before going to Minnesota. I knew that I would miss being away from my parents and my brothers and sisters, but I had the opportunity to play baseball and get paid for doing it."

The young man from Alabama was a long way from home. Now he was going to see new territory. In fact, Al had no idea where Minnesota was located on the map. He said, "Dick told me that I was to ride with him. I was so lost, if he would have dropped me off anywhere along the route, I don't know if I ever would have found my way back home to Alabama."

Al stayed in a private home where he was charged $1 a night. He said that he did not eat his meals there but it was a nice place. He tells about his southern accent being hard to understand by the northerners. He said, "I went into a café and ordered a cold drink, the waitress brought me a glass of cold water. I told her that I didn't want a glass of cold water but I wanted a cold drink." "Oh," she said, "then you want a pop."

"That really confused me. The only thing I knew about pop was that he was my dad. I told her that I never heard that word used for a cold drink. She looked at me and laughed, saying, 'You want a soda'. Having said that, she went and brought me a coke. What a tough time I had trying to buy a coke."

"The Fulda team was made up of local players," said Al. "There were four of us who were hired from the outside to play. It wasn't at all like playing for Metter, Georgia. The caliber of play seemed better. Our team needed a shortstop so I told them about my brother-in-law who married my sister, Evelynn. I wanted my sister there to cook for us! The owner hired him and he brought Evelynn with him. I didn't realize how home sick I was for my family. Their presence really made me feel a lot better.

What a time we had. I lived with my sister and her husband in the back of a mortuary. The owner had the caskets in the front room. I didn't want anyone to think that I was uneasy but I must admit I kept an eye on those caskets. I don't think I would have stayed there alone. I was especially thankful for my sister and her husband. I remember we could look through a hole in the floor and see the mortician work on the bodies. The apartment was nice even if we could see through the hole into the basement."

The temperature was much colder then they were used to in Alabama. Al slept with a heavy sweatshirt on. At the ballpark, the people came with their coats and blankets. Most of the nights were quite chilly.

"Do you like cornbread, Allan?" Asked Mrs. Roundhorse, a board member's wife. I have a pan of it to eat with fish."

"I got the idea immediately that Mrs. Roundhorse expected me to eat the whole thing. I didn't like cornbread that well back then but I took it not wanting to hurt Mrs. Roundhorse's feelings. I finally gave it away to some others at the fish fry."

Some dreams do come true. As Al looked back on his life with its many twists and turns, he could see the hand of God working in his behalf even though he did not personally know the Lord during those years. Regarding that span of years, he said, "There is no doubt but what God had His hand on my life. I was not totally clean but I wasn't really bad either. All I know is that I purposely never turned against the Lord. I had too much fear of a Holy God to do that.

Going to Fulda was not a coincidence," remarked Al with that telling smile on his face. "When Frank Lary directed Dick Reusse to come and talk with me about playing for Fulda, that was not coincidence either. I believe God had me in the right place at the right time even though that was not my thinking at the time."

Shirley was a student at Saint Catherines in St. Paul. She was home from college. She taught swimming during the summer at the local lake for the Red Cross. She excelled in swimming. Going back in his thoughts to that important time in his life, Al said, "Her uncle, Dick Reusse, introduced me to her. She was about five feet tall and very pretty. We hit it off right away. Some people laugh at the possibility of love at first sight. As for me, I believe, with Shirley, it was love at first sight. The love was young and would grow-which it did. That pretty little lady from Fulda occupied my thoughts and dreams like I never thought could be possible."

Al said that he was shy in his high school days and that shyness followed him through college and to Fulda. He said, "Shirley and I began to date. She found out immediately that I didn't talk very much and especially in public. Shirley did not have that same shyness when it came to talking. It would have been a catastrophe if she did. She talked enough for the two of us at first. I would just sit and listen. She was so pretty and such an intelligent conversationalist, it was a joy to be in her company. We had a wonderful time the rest of the summer. I enjoyed eating at her house which was often."

The southern accent provided more laughs for Shirley's family. Al kept the phone line quite busy from where he lived to the Reusse house. It got to the place where Mrs. Reusse didn't have to understand what Al was saying. She recognized his voice and knew the call was for Shirley. He even surprised Shirley's mother one day by singing the song, "Alabama, Alabama" on the phone. Over 50 years later, Al said one day he spoke on the phone with his mother-in-law and she understood him for the first time.

"Getting to know the Reusse family was a lot of fun," said Al. "One time Shirley asked me what I would like to eat. I told her that I would be pleased to have rice. That evening there was a dish of something on the table. When I asked Shirley what it was, she said it was rice. It was Spanish (red) rice. I was embarrassed for asking for it. At the meal when I ate about 12 slices of bread, Shirley's family seemed surprised. What they didn't know was that feeding us bread was one way my mother filled us up.

Talk about being different," Al went on, "When I got a job helping to build houses, I found out I could drive in nails with either hand. I shave left-handed, eat with my left hand, shoot a gun from my left side, and put my belt on from the left side. From my right side, I pitch, kick, and write.

I found myself less and less homesick for Alabama after I met Shirley. We had so much fun together. She even helped me with my shyness and before I realized what was happening, I was talking with others very easily."

Even the game of baseball took on a different view for Al. With Shirley watching from the stands, her presence seemed to give him encouragement. They only knew each other for a short time but he knew he loved her and that she loved him. It even made playing ball that much more enjoyable.

Al said he did not remember much about his involvement in baseball that summer. Several things, however, did stand out in his memory. He said, "I remember a game against Wilmont. It was on a Sunday night and there was a big crowd present. The longer the game went, the stronger I felt. I pitched a no-hitter that night. I did walk two batters and hit one. We won by the score of 3 to 0."

60

Dick Reusse, Shirley's uncle and promotion manager for the Fulda Giants in the First Night League, reported that summer that at least three members of his team would be signing contracts with major league teams. This only confirmed that the Fulda Giants was a quality team and played a good caliber of baseball.

Another thing that Al mentioned was the time they went to Iona to play. "The town where the team was located had a population of about 400 people. When the game started, there were approximately 5,000 people on hand. I had no idea where they came from but they showed up to cheer for their team and cheer they did.

I became a closer friend to Dick," said Al. "After all, he hired me to play for the Fulda Giants. The best thing that Dick ever did for me was to introduce me to his niece, Shirley. Another thing that I recall about Dick was when we played away from home I always rode with him. After the game, we always stopped at a steak house. The thing I liked about that was that Dick always paid for the meal. You can't beat that to have your boss chauffeur you to and from the games and to buy your meals as well. There is nothing that tastes better than a Minnesota steak. I became a good steak eater which meant that as my family grew; they too, learned to eat and like steaks."

Al loved to talk about the past and growing up in Fulton Springs and Inglenook. He said that one of the teachings of his mama that stuck with him was to address people properly. He said, "a friend of mine in Fulda, named John Tusseth owned a department store. One day he said, "Al, don't you like me?" I responded and said that I did like him. He continued, "Then call me John and not Mr. Tusseth." I thought for a moment and told him that I couldn't do that, Mr. Tusseth was 60 years old and I was 22. I told him that my mother had taught me to say Sir or Mr. and Madam. My mother's instructions as well as warnings stuck with me like glue through out the years."

61

10

GOODBYE SHIRLEY - HELLO DETROIT

"George Moriarity was a scout for the Detroit Tigers. He watched me pitch a game and came to talk with me. He told me, "I don't need to see you pitch anymore. I want you to go to Detroit and let them have a look at you." He said the Tigers would pay my transportation from Minneapolis to Detroit and then home to Alabama. I asked him if he was sure of what he was telling me because I had a ride back to Alabama with my sister and brother-in-law. He assured me that the Detroit baseball club would reimburse me for the sleeper. That night from Minneapolis to Detroit was the first time I slept in a bed on a train. There was a big lump in my throat when I said goodbye to Shirley. That was a hard thing to do. She encouraged me by saying that she would come to see me next summer no matter where I played ball."

The night in the sleeper railroad car was not a restful one for Al. The train went through Chicago. Al was not sure but he thought his sleeper was switched to another train. He arrived in Detroit and was put up at the Cadillac Hotel. John McHale, who played limited ball for the Tigers, was assigned to look after Al. Knowing he would be seeing the Tigers play, Al asked George Moriarity to ask the Detroit club if he could pitch batting practice. "I guess," he said, "they didn't think that was a good idea. While in Detroit, I saw a three game series with the New York Yankees. I saw big Johnny Mize hit three home runs in one game. This is what I have heard called the big leagues. They sure played good ball. I remember seeing Vic Wertz, a power hitter, wearing a guard on his right leg. He batted left-handed and was walked a number of times. A power hitter is always a threat. I had not heard of Vic Wertz before that time but I could see why they walked him. He could really hit the ball.

One of the players for the Tigers was Frank House who was a catcher for Bessemer High School in Bessemer, Alabama. I pitched against Frank when I was playing for Phillips High. Frank eventually played ten years in the majors with a .248 batting average. One night, Frank and a friend of his took me to see a boxing match between Jack LaMotta and a boxer from France. The match ended in the 15th round when LaMotta scored a knockout."

Al wondered if he would get the opportunity to pitch. Red Rolfe, who played third base for the New York Yankees from 1934 to 1942, was the manager for Detroit. Al describes what took place. "The manager did not let me throw batting practice. Instead, Joe Ginsberg, a catcher, was assigned to catch me. Throwing to a batter is a lot different than warming up to a catcher. To be honest about it, throwing to Joe Ginsberg did not do much for me. After about 10 or 15 minutes, Red Rolfe stopped me and said, "Son, your ball goes the wrong way. You go back home and we will have our scout in Alabama look at you and get that ball to go the right direction."

"I felt terrible inside. I knew what I was capable of doing with a ball in my hand. I looked at the manager and thought how unreasonable he was. It was not possible for my fastball to do anything else other than what it always does. It slides and sinks naturally. Today, if I could still throw, it would do the same things that Joe Ginsberg saw it do when he caught me.

All I can say is that Detroit didn't want me and they certainly were not nice to me as far as showing them what I could do when facing batters. The next day I checked with the Tigers' office before I checked out of the hotel. I was told that my way from Minneapolis to Birmingham would not be paid like their scout, George Moriarity, told me. The man in the office said that the ball club would only pay my way to Detroit and back to Chicago."

Al was between a rock and a hard place. When he told the office man that the scout told him that his return trip would be paid by the Detroit club all the way to Alabama, the man told him, "We will not pay your way. If the Tigers had wanted me, they would have been glad to pay my way home."

After hearing all of that, Al said that it was the first time in his life that he felt like hurting someone. The check they gave him for transportation to Chicago was an insult to Al. He said, "I was so frustrated and hurt that I wanted to open his mouth and jam that check down his throat. First, I was being treated like a kid who didn't know any thing about pitching and second, I was being lied to and mistreated for something that was not of my doing."

It cost Al $60 to fly to Birmingham. What happened in Detroit regarding the poor treatment on the field and the fiasco in the office really bothered the young pitcher. He wrote to George Moriarity sharing with him what had taken place. The scout said he was disappointed.

Coach "Happy" Campbell of the University of Alabama had called Al even before he left for Detroit. He asked him to come back and play football for the Crimson Tide. Al told him that his left shoulder was still not well enough to play football. He was told to come back and block with his right shoulder.

Later on when Al walked on the football field at the University, he watched the practice for about ten minutes. He said, "I walked off the field and never looked back. I have never missed football since." He went on to say, "All these stories about players taking easy courses were certainly true in my case. I took woodwork, sheet metal work and first aid. In religion class, I cheated on tests. As I look back I feel so badly about it all. How many times have people said that they would like to live areas of their life over again? I have felt like that but we know it is impossible to do. We can definitely learn from those experiences and profit by them."

II

WEDDING BELLS
IN FULDA

Allan Fulton Worthington was in love. The five-foot tall college student and swimming instructor in Fulda, Minnesota had swept the six foot two, 200-pound young man off his feet. He found himself day dreaming more and more about Shirley. He visualized her sitting in the stands cheering for him. He thought of the times they would sit and talk over two glasses of coke. Her pretty face and cute smile seemed so real that it made his heart skip a beat. How thankful the two were for telephones. Al felt his life would never be complete without Shirley being a part of it. His thoughts, talk and plans involved the sweet swimming instructor from Fulda in the state of ten thousand lakes. "Shirley and I spent a lot of time on the telephone," said Al. "She didn't have any problem understanding my southern accent like her mother did. I kept myself broke just talking on the phone. It was that fall in early September when I proposed to her over the telephone. In spite of my shyness, I got the words out of my mouth in the right order. I can still hear her wonderful response of "yes." I was walking on air at that moment. I wrote to her parents asking for their daughter's hand in marriage. They, too, said yes. Shirley began immediately to make plans for our wedding."

Excitement hardly describes Al's thoughts of getting married to Shirley Reusse. He got her ring size and purchased an engagement ring as well as a wedding ring. Al wanted his bride to be to have her ring and to wear the engagement ring immediately. "I'm sending the ring by mail," he told Shirley. "I want you to start wearing the engagement ring as soon as you receive it."

December that year was especially cold at home in Alabama. Since their wedding date was scheduled for December 28 Al decided to leave and spend Christmas in Fulda. He left by bus from Birmingham on December 20. Before leaving, however, he dressed as warmly as he could. He said he put on two pairs of socks and his feet still felt frozen during the two days of travel.

Shirley asked her father if she could drive the car to Fairmount, Minnesota to pick Al up at the bus station. She was given permission to take the car. She picked up Al and the two started the return trip to Fulda. There was ice and snow on the road making it very difficult to drive.

"We began to skid on the ice," Al said as he described the accident. "We ended up sliding into a ditch that was filled with snow. The car turned over onto its roof and bounced up again and when we stopped, the car was facing Fairmount. Shirley was crying and I thought I might cheer her up by laughing. It was a strange scene. We began to assess any damage done to us. Shirley had a few minor cuts and I came out of it without a scratch."

"What do we do now?" asked Shirley wiping the tears from her face.

"There isn't much we can do," answered Al. "We'll just wait until someone comes along who can help us."

Al thought how pretty Shirley looked even with her tear stained face. Before long, a farmer appeared. He attached a chain to the car and pulled it back on the road.

"It was in pretty bad shape," Al remarked. "None of the doors shut tight. It was bent up a lot. I turned the ignition key and the engine started and ran well. We thanked the farmer and headed for Fulda."

When Al and Shirley arrived back at Shirley's home, her father was quite upset because of the accident and the damage done to the car, a 1949 Ford which was to be a wedding gift for Al and Shirley. "I have a friend who runs a repair shop," said Dad Reusse. "He'll be able to fix it." They used the car to pull their house trailer for a couple of years and many miles.

"I sure started that important visit to my future in-laws with a bang. I nearly froze getting to Fairmount, Minnesota, by bus and then was in the car accident with my bride to be on our way to Fulda. I wondered what next was in store for me before our wedding date."

It was a very cold day with the temperature 20 degrees below zero. Dad Reusse thought it would be a good day to go ice fishing and asked Al to go with him. Al said jokingly that the most ice he had seen were the cubes in the tray in the refrigerator. He broke out laughing as he described the fishing experience.

"We went in Mr. Reusse's truck and drove to Round Lake. It was located at the town of Worthington about 17 miles from Fulda. I was a little concerned that driving out on the ice with the truck might chalk up another mishap on my visit to Minnesota. Shirley's dad assured me that the ice was thick enough to hold us. I could not believe how many cars and trucks were out on the lake. There were people all over the place with small tents to protect them from the cold and wind.

When Dad Reusse started out on the ice, I opened the truck door just in case we would break through the ice. We found a hole where someone else had been. We put up our icehouse and started fishing. I thought all we lacked was a heater.

When we finally came out of the tent house, all the cars and trucks were gone. A storm was coming so we left quickly. I didn't say anything to Dad Reusse but I was sure glad to get off that lake and get back to a warm house."

Another experience that Al had in those days at Shirley's house just prior to their wedding was when he went hunting with her dad. "Come on, Al, I'm going to take you hunting," said Mr. Reusse. "Do you like to hunt?"

He then tossed a shirt and coat to Al to put on. Al thought to himself that no way was he going to go out in 20 degrees below zero without several layers of clothing. He went and put on two more sweatshirts. He said he wore that much sometimes-in 50 degrees above zero back in Alabama. The two men were soon off in the truck that had a heater but it wasn't working. They got to the hunting area and started walking in the deep snow. The next thing Al knew, he was beginning to perspire all over his body. The way things were going for Al that week he would not have been surprised if he shot himself in the foot. The knee-deep snow was a real challenge for the young man from the South. The ride back home in the cold truck was almost too much for Al to take with his wet clothes. The big guy had mixed emotions. He wanted more than anything else to be with Shirley and her parents but he sure could have gone without the cold trip North, the wreck between Fairmount and Fulda, the nerve shaking fishing trip, and the hunting trek through the knee-deep snow in 20-degrees below zero temperature with sweat-soaked clothing.

"Besides the car, which we wrecked," spoke Al in a serious voice. "Shirley's mom and dad also gave us a tremendous gift of $500. Things were looking much better. For one thing, there wasn't time for any more fishing or hunting trips. My dad, mother, Charles, and Edna Earle arrived by car for the wedding. It was wonderful to have them there.

My dear mother was her usual self. One day she was talking among a group of some ten women about her trip to Minnesota and the beautiful scenery she enjoyed while riding along. She said, "When we were coming through Iowa, those barns were prettier than my house back in Alabama." I thought that's my mama. She says it like it is, no matter how it sounds."

The night before the wedding, Al slept at Shirley's Uncle Carl's house. In the middle of the night he was still wide-awake and wanted to get up and do some jogging. He was nervous, scared and anxious, all at the same time. He wondered if every man about to be married felt the same way.

One thing Al knew for sure, he was marrying a religious girl. Shirley was Catholic and was very faithful in attending church. Al was happy that he was marrying a girl who went to church. He said that he was not a regular churchgoer at this time. He also said that he had no idea what the Catholic Church believed and taught. He did recall how back in Inglenook, when he was a boy, the one and only Catholic Church had field days or fun days. In the field alongside the church, he said, they played all kinds of games throughout the fun days.

"My marriage to Shirley was, of course, a major step in my life that brought about major changes," commented Al. "We were married on December 28, 1950 in the Catholic Church where Shirley was reared. The wedding ceremony was a simple one. That pretty little swimming instructor became my wife. Within two days, we left Fulda for Alabama."

12

DISAPPOINTMENT IN ATLANTA

"I was in the National Guard. Someone said at school that if we joined the National Guard, we would not be drafted. Shirley and I had an apartment in Tuscaloosa on the second floor. The downstairs was vacant. It was dark and scary. When we returned to the apartment after dark, we had to walk in the dark house and go up the dark stairway. I don't know why there weren't any lights lit. It cost us $50 a month and I thought that was pretty good. I was paid $75 a month by the school because I did not eat or sleep on campus."

"The spring was hard on Shirley because I had to leave her alone while I went off and played ball for the University. It was

February 1951 and both Shirley and I realized that married life was not what we had expected as far as not being together most of the time. She became very lonely and hated to be alone, cooped up in the apartment while I had to attend classes, practice, and play ball. Her parents came down to visit us which was a big help to Shirley."

Before they were married Al's National Guard unit was called up for active duty. He was suddenly called up for a physical exam for the army. He was standing in the line before an army doctor who spotted the scar from the operation on his left shoulder. He said, "We can't use you." That was like music to Al's ears. Wanting to sound disappointed, he responded, "You can't use me?" Al got dressed and went back home.

He found out the National Guard had turned his name over to the draft board because he skipped out on the two weeks of camp he was supposed to attend in the summer. Instead, he went to play baseball.

"When the 1951 spring semester was coming to a close," said Al, "I was at the draft board headquarters one day pleading my case. I was supposed to leave for the army by June 2. I said to the lady behind the desk, "Ma'am, I don't mind going into the army, but could I wait and go in the month of September? You see, ma'am, I just got married several months ago and I need to make some money."

If looks could kill, I would be dead now, he thought. She looked at me with her best ugly look and said, "Son, we have been waiting on you a long time. Come June 2, you are gone!"

Her ugly look turned to a happy expression when she told me that. "I said, Lady, is there any way I can get out of going?"

She gave me that ugly look again and said, "You can get out of going if your wife is pregnant."

Al interrupted her right there and said, "Lady, shake my hand! My wife just told me this morning that she is pregnant."

The lady's chin dropped to her chest. She finally looked up at me and said, "Bring me a letter from the doctor confirming the fact that your wife is going to have a baby."

"I'll be right back," I responded with a smile on my face and a spring in my steps. "Thank you, Shirley," I whispered as I left that office. I had the doctor's letter in the lady's hands in record time."

Al's troubles were not over yet. He was called into the Registrar's office at the University and was notified that he had missed every special meeting he was supposed to attend. The registrar said, "I can't believe that you have been here for three and one half years and not attended even one meeting." Al said later that he really didn't have any interest in going to the meetings.

"He then got my transcript out," said Al, "and looked hard and long at my terrible grades."

He raised his voice a bit as he spoke. "How have you managed to stay in school as long as you have with grades like these? You should be doing something good for society. Go out and help build buildings!" Before our meeting was ended, we both had to laugh.

"The coming weekend we had a scheduled game with Vanderbilt. Because the paper work on me would not be in before Monday, he permitted me to go ahead and play that last game of the season. I pitched my last game for Alabama in Nashville, Tennessee. The opposing pitcher for Vanderbilt was Bill Wade, a good friend, who was later an outstanding quarterback for the Chicago Bears. It was a windy day but we finally won the game."

After the game, Al saw Coach Campbell in the hotel and asked him, "Coach, do you think you could get me signed up with a team in pro ball?"

Coach Campbell looked at Al and said, "Get you signed up the way you pitched today?

Al went on to say that he found it hard to pitch in cold windy weather. When he returned to Tuscaloosa, he and Shirley left the university. The father-to-be really felt bad that he had not given his best in his studies. The university had supported him for three and one half years. In acknowledging his failure as a student, Al said, "When I think of the many young men who would have given most anything to have had the wonderful opportunities that I had and wasted them. I am not proud of the fact that I could be one of the worst students, academically that attended the University of Alabama. I am not at all proud of that."

Al and Shirley went to Birmingham for a few days before going on to play semi-pro ball again for a town called Wasaco in Minnesota. While in Birmingham, Al pitched for Stockham. This was the team that he had wished he was good enough to play with but never did until this point. Frank Lary who was Al's teammate for the Crimson Tide was pitching for the opposing team. Frank was in the army at the time.

"We won the game," remarked Al, "and I got two hits off Frank. I felt pretty good about that."

Young Al was looking for an opening to get into professional baseball. He was even willing to stall a bit before going to Minnesota and try all possibilities. In his numerous contacts, Al told about an elderly man named Bill. He could not remember Bill's last name but he said that Bill was a bird dog scout for the Atlanta Cracker's, a minor league baseball team. Bill asked Al to go with him to Atlanta for a work out to see if they might be interested in him.

Fred (Dixie) Walker, who played eighteen years in the major leagues was the manager for the Atlanta ball club. Dixie won the national league batting title in 1944 with a .357 average. "We took the bus to Atlanta and went to the ball park," Al said, "This to me was big time baseball. I asked Bill to talk with the right people to see if I could pitch batting practice."

Dixie Walker looked at Al and asked, "How old are you?" Al told him that he was 21 years old. Dixie then said, "You look older than that to me." Al kept quiet and didn't say anything. He was actually 22 years old.

Dixie did not allow Al to pitch batting practice but did allow him to warm up on the side while he spoke to Earl Mann, the General Manager of the Atlanta Club. The determined young Al felt that Dixie did not want him. Later on, Al went up to the General Manager's office. He knocked and was told to enter. "When I entered," said Al, "I walked over toward his desk. Without raising his head, he said, "You wasted four years in going to college when you could have been playing ball."

Al was taken by surprise by the General Manager's remarks. The meeting ended without much more said, Al left the office and found Bill. When a scout takes a prospect to work out with a team, it is customary to buy a steak or nice dinner for the prospect. In this case, Bill bought Al a hot dog when they entered the stadium, and another when they left, just before Al caught the bus to Birmingham.

13

OPPORTUNITY AT SULPHUR DELL

Dickey Martin, a manager of one of the teams Al played against in the South wanted to help him catch on with a professional baseball club. He knew Larry Gilbert, the owner and general manager of the Nashville Vols, a team in double A ball in the Southern Association. "Dickey wanted me to work out with Nashville," said Al, "so Larry Gilbert paid my air fare to Mobile where the Vols were playing the Mobile Bears at the time.

Upon arriving, I asked if I could throw batting practice. I felt if I got the opportunity to throw batting practice, there would be a good chance of the Nashville Club signing me because I was confident the batters would not hit me."

The Nashville lineup was filled with left-handed hitters and that was in Al's favor. He loved to pitch against batters hitting from the left side. Even though Al was a right-hander, his fastball moved in on the hands of left-handed batters. The big right-hander did not want to throw too hard because he did not want any of the Nashville batters to think of him as a college hotdog.

Al remarked later, "The whole batting practice was like a pepper game. The batters kept hitting the ball back to the mound. If I have to say so myself, I believe the manager, coaches and even the players liked what they saw."

Not too much was said to Al except that he did a good job. Without the promise of a contract, he and Shirley planned to leave for Wasaco, Minnesota, where Al would play semi-pro ball for $600 a month. Before they left, Larry Gilbert of the Nashville Vols called and asked Al to come by Nashville on their way to Minnesota. They stopped off in Nashville to see the General Manager and liked what they heard from him.

"This is the opportunity you've been waiting for, Al," said Shirley. "I would be closer to my parents in Minnesota but this is more important to the both of us."

Al signed a contract for $400 a month and received a $1,500 bonus for signing. Larry Gilbert also had written in the contract that Al would get one fourth of the selling price if the Nashville Club sold him in the future.

Referring to the caliber of baseball in the Southern Association, Al called it a strong league. He said, "I had no idea how I would do overall. I think Mr. Gilbert allowed me to work out with his team because a few years earlier, Mr. Martin called him about giving a work out opportunity to a pitcher, Bubba Church. Mr. Gilbert said Bubba did not throw hard enough but Bubba Church later pitched in the majors for six years."

Allan Fulton Worthington had joined the ranks of many before him. He was employed as a professional baseball player. His first pitching assignment as a Nashville Vol was against his hometown team, the Birmingham Barons. Al could not help but think that he would be pitching against a team that did not show any interest in signing him.

He said, "It seemed like all my family was in Nashville at Sulphur Dell baseball stadium that night I pitched against Birmingham. I won my first professional baseball game by beating the Barons by the score of 8 – 5. I could not have been any happier had I pitched a no-hitter. We were a very happy family that night."

The day after he won over Birmingham, Shirley flew to Sioux Falls, South Dakota, where her family, with whom she stayed two weeks, met her. At the end of two weeks, Al went to get her and they drove back to Nashville together.

On their trip to Tennessee, he ran at times on the highway ahead of the car while Shirley followed close behind. "I had to get my running in somehow," said Al.

One thing Al found out quickly was that the double A hitters would not chase many bad balls. The 1951 season ended with him winning seven games and losing ten. He was told that to be good, he needed to win seven out of ten games. He had some improving to do. He was not overwhelmed with joy about his season but it was not a disaster either. He was eagerly looking forward to the 1952 season.

With the season over, Al and Shirley started out by car to spend the winter with her parents. At one point in their trip, they were part of a line of vehicles following a slow moving truck up a long grade. All the other vehicles finally got around the truck except Al and Shirley and the car in front of them. Finally the car ahead of them moved out to go around the truck. Al followed close behind but not being able to see the road ahead. The car ahead of him moved over in front of the truck it had just passed. Straight ahead coming toward them was a car traveling very fast. There was no way for Al to get out of the way of the oncoming car. At the last moment, the car ran off the road narrowly missing Al and Shirley and then turned back on the road behind them.

"That close call taught me a lesson about driving that I will always remember," said Al. "We both could have lost our lives very easily. I believe with all my heart that God's hand was upon us even though at the time, neither of us knew Him as our Heavenly Father."

Going to Minnesota for the winter gave Al mixed feelings. It was hard for him to forget the fishing trip out on the ice and the knee-deep snow hunting experience. He loved to be with Shirley's family but he sure didn't like their cold weather. The closer he and Shirley got to Fulda, the more he thought he could smell those special cinnamon rolls that Mom Reusse baked for him. O course it was only in Al's mind, but he claimed to have a good imagination. As a matter of fact, Al enjoyed everything his mother-in-law baked or cooked.

"I did what many ball players did in the winter," said Al with his familiar grin. "I took up duck and pheasant hunting. Of course, if something else came within range, I probably would take a shot at it."

Shirley's dad made a blind in the lake the family owned. The name of it was Badger Lake. He was an expert in shooting game birds and he loved to hunt. I have always been a late sleeper but Dad Reusse put a stop to that when it came to hunting. At 4 a.m. he would come to the bed and punch me on the shoulder. That meant just one thing; get up now!

We didn't even eat breakfast and that broke another rule for me. I always had to have a good breakfast before I left the house. Dad was a good shot and he proved it by the many ducks he would get. Most of the ducks were green head mallards. What a fun time it was to come back to the house after our morning hunt with our catch and sit down to a delicious Mom Reusse breakfast of eggs, bacon, toast and coffee. Oh yes, I don't want to forget the cinnamon rolls. Then to the living room for a nap after the cold morning hunting."

Some of the Reusse relatives came from St Paul on the weekends and always returned home with a supply of duck meat. Al thought the best time to shoot ducks was when they migrated south from Canada and Northern Minnesota. For some reason, Al said, many of the ducks flew low over the lake. They shot so much, the gun barrels got hot and stayed that way during the shooting.

Al learned a number of things that winter and one of them was how to clean ducks.

"To help us out that winter, I got a job delivering furniture," Al said. "The store was owned by three men, Paul, Fritz and Carl, all brothers. Paul was my father-in-law. I usually went with Fritz. He was a happy fellow and always smiling. One day he told me that he could not stand to hear a preacher preach. However, they were a religious family. Fritz's wife was a Lutheran and a fine woman. Fritz was a Catholic as were his children. When it came down to it," said Al, "I wasn't anything."

Lawrence Welk got his start on the second floor of their furniture store. They danced in the store after pushing the furniture against the walls. Lawrence Welk was a young musician from Sioux Falls, South Dakota.

14

MOTHER SHIRLEY AND DAUGHTER LINDA

The day finally arrived for Shirley. The pains she was having gave a clear signal that she soon would become a mother. She was taken to a hospital in not too distant Worthington. On October 7, 1951 tiny Linda arrived weighing four pounds, six ounces. Because she was six week premature, she had to remain at the hospital. She was the first Worthington to be born in Worthington, Minnesota. Al and Shirley made daily trips to Worthington to see their precious daughter. It was difficult for them to be separated from her but they knew it was the best thing to do.

The day the happy couple brought her home was a day of rejoicing and thanksgiving. The pretty tiny Linda had center stage in the Reusse home. Nearly every sound she made brought an immediate response from someone. Al and Shirley were especially thankful for the $1,500 bonus paid to Al for signing with Nashville. He felt so good and relieved that he had a professional baseball club to return to in the spring.

Unknown to Al, he had a shock waiting for him. Al describes the shock he received when Baby Linda was brought home from the hospital. His sweetheart, Shirley, informed him beyond any doubt what his new responsibilities were regarding little Linda. They fixed up a crib with two lights under it to help keep Linda warm. "Honey," said Shirley looking up at her tall handsome husband, "Our baby belongs to both of us. She must be fed every two hours and she will also have to have her diapers changed. I just know you'll enjoy doing these things for her and me."

"Shirley could not have said it any better and I could not have understood it any better either," said the proud father. "If I must say so myself, I got pretty good in making Linda's formulas, heating it to the right temperature, and changing her diapers. As the Lord gave us children, I can say that I changed diapers for all of them.

It was enjoyable staying the winter with Mom and Dad Reusse. We had a lot of fun telling stories. I reminded them of the time when they came down to visit us at Tuscaloosa, Alabama during the 1951 college baseball season. They stayed with us in the second floor apartment that was looking better to us as the days went by. One day while in Orlando to play Rollins College, we went to Daytona Beach and stayed one night there.

Shirley and I went swimming. I had on a long-flannel-shirt that came down to my knees. We stayed in the water and on the beach for a good five hours. At the end of the day, you could have fried an egg on my back. I had a terrible sunburn. The next day I had to pitch against Rollins College in Orlando. Talk about tears, every time I bent down or even moved, it hurt so bad I was weeping silently. I was really miserable. Coach Campbell was not sympathetic at all. He simply said, "That will teach you to lay in the sun." "You can be sure that I learned that lesson well.

On the way to Orlando from Alabama, we saw some orange groves. It was getting dark but the trees along side the road were still visible. We drove right into the orange grove. We left the lights on and got out and helped ourselves. As far as I know, mom and dad may have thought the oranges grew wild or they were free. I didn't have the heart to say anything to these foreigners from Minnesota. It was the first time they were south of Denver."

As Al, Shirley, and her parents sat around the table and did some reminiscing, the room was filled with laughter. All of a sudden there was a tiny cry from baby Linda. Shirley looked over at Al. No words were spoken. He knew it was his turn to feed and diaper.

The weather in Minnesota was beginning to get cold. Al thought a lot of the 60-degree temperature in Alabama but it didn't help him one bit. One evening Shirley asked Al to go ice-skating. It was so cold that Al's nose became numb. He said the city cleaned the snow off part of the ice on the lake. Not being used to skating, he stayed quite close to the edge of the snow. When he felt like he was going to go down he would jump into the snow to give him stability.

After struggling around on the ice for a while which was too long for big Al, the two sat down to take off their skates and to put on more comfortable footwear as far as Al was concerned. Being born and raised in Minnesota, Shirley was no stranger to ice-skating. She certainly was no match in trying to keep her husband on his skates. In his memory logbook, Al chalked up the ice skating event as just a fun time of balancing. He never skated again.

They returned to the house just in time for Al's turn for feeding and changing Linda. He never had any idea what mothers did to keep on top of all their responsibilities in caring for their babies. Al would be the first to give honor where honor is due. In this case, it would be his dear sweet wife, Shirley. There was no stopping his love and deep respect for the wonderful mate the Lord gave to him.

When Linda began sleeping through most of the night without needing her bottle, that good change in her schedule did not cause any problem for her daddy. Al was fully content in getting that extra shuteye. The family of three was fused together with a love that could not be described by words. Every day seemed more precious then the previous day.

Then, too, it was wonderful to be with Mom and Dad Reusse. Any question that daughter Shirley had regarding baby Linda could be answered by her mother. Al and Shirley could not have had a better environment in which to live those early months with baby Linda.

15

GOOD NEWS FROM NASHVILLE

"One day the mailman delivered a letter from Larry Gilbert," said Al. "I opened it to find a contract for $400 a month. I wrote back and asked him to raise it to $500. We wrote back and forth. One of his letters said that I was in the wrong league. He finally offered me a contract for $450 per month that I signed. He later wrote me a letter telling me not to bring my wife to spring training camp in Melbourne, Florida, because there was no place for wives to stay.

This was my first spring training camp and I did not want to go without Shirley and Linda. Shirley's dad went to the bank and signed a note for $1,500. A man in town had a 27-foot trailer that was like new. We bought it and started out in a snowstorm. In Worthington, where Linda was born, we went around a big curve. Shirley and I looked out the window to see our trailer whipping around along side us. You don't have to ask me if we were scared. We were petrified with fear. I got it back where it was supposed to be and we continued on our way. I am talking about February weather in Minnesota. That first day we traveled only 150 miles and stayed in a motel that night.

The next morning we found our trailer wheels were frozen to the ground. We got them thawed and started off again. It was another bad day of traveling with another 150 miles traveled. Something had to change. We had to make better time then what we had been doing. Once we got out of the snow and on dry pavement, we did a lot better."

When Al and Shirley arrived in Melbourne with baby Linda, Shirley was the only wife there. Al had written Larry Gilbert telling him that he was bringing his wife and also his own house. They found a nice trailer park along the beach. It was a beautiful place. They especially enjoyed the shrimp that were plentiful on a daily basis. They purchased the delicacy directly from the fishermen, who caught them. There was a bridge nearby where the fishermen with their lamps and nets, would catch shrimp during the night. Al and Shirley bought all they wanted for three cents apiece.

The 1952 baseball season was not a bad season for Al. He received a lot of press in the Nashville Tennessean and the Nashville Banner. On Saturday morning, April 19, 1952, the Vols stood in the standings at 3 wins and 2 losses in the young season. Just the night before, Al handed his hometown Birmingham Barons a white washing, 4 to 0. Russ Melvin, the Tennessean Sports writer called it a masterful three-hit performance. The Vol's manager, Hugh Poland, said he hoped the rest of the pitching staff would follow suit. Al not only shut out the Barons but he helped his own cause by banging out a double.

In talking about his pitching against Birmingham, Al said, "I'll be faster later on when the weather gets warmer. Not that I wouldn't take one like this anytime. But I want to control my curve a bit better and I feel I want to put more on my fast ball when the weather warms up and I work more often."

Larry Gilbert, the Vol's General Manager, said the thing that impressed him most was the way Al mowed down the side on strikes in the eighth inning. He ended his comments by saying, "There's no telling how far this boy can go."

The 1952 season was a tremendous learning season for Al. He had some of the finest hitters in the league behind him. Sluggers like Bama Ray, Dusty Rhodes, Rance Press, Bob Lennon, Bob Boring and Jim Marshall, had the power to knock the ball out of any baseball stadium.

While Al was away with the team, Shirley kept the home fires burning. The players' wives are a very special group of people. They feel the disappointments and the happiness their husbands feel. Concerning Al's road trips from home, Shirley said, "You never get used to his being away, no matter how many trips there are."

When Al was having a bit of trouble with his pitching in the early part of the 1952 season, Shirley said that she and Allan had worried considerably over his difficulties. They both felt a lot better when the problems seemed to be ironing out.

She said, "I've been in the stands watching him when fans around me were saying all sorts of uncomplimentary things about him. But I can honestly say, I just shrug it off. When I married Al, my dad warned me I'd hear these things but not to pay any attention. And he was right. The fans pay for the privilege of saying what they please, providing it isn't personally insulting."

Wedding Day
December 28, 1950

Al with son Marshal

Al & Shirley

Ice Skating in Fulda

Al with Marshal and
Daniel

The Worthington Family 1968
Allan, Michele, Daniel, Al, Marshal, Shirley, Linda

Al and Shirley in 2003

Fifty Happy Years

Family at 50th Anniversary Celebration

Worthington Family

Al with son Al

Al
Shirley
Michele
Marshal
Daniel

Worthington Family
Al, Shirley, Marshal, Linda, Allan, Daniel, Michele,
and Phyllis the poodle

16

FIRST FULL SEASON
IN PRO BALL

With the 1952 season ended, it marked Al's first full season in professional baseball. He had made the connection with pro ball that he had worked so hard to do. The disappointing Detroit and Atlanta experiences were in the past. Once Al signed with Nashville, he was hopeful of having a job somewhere in professional baseball in the future. The first hurdle of being signed is where many promising young men stop. Al was on his way and was confirming what many knowledgeable baseball men and sports writers had said about him. He was not only known around the Southern Association League cities but there were those in Major League front offices who were taking notice of him, as well.

Al was quite happy with his 1952 achievements. He said, "When the season ended, I finished with 13 wins and 13 losses. I led the league in strike outs, hit batsmen, walks, and wild pitches." He believed that he could get fewer losses in 1953 as well as reduce the numbers in hit batsmen, walks and wild pitches.

He went on to say, "I won a Bulova watch in Nashville for pitching a shutout. It was a rain shortened six innings. Anyone who pitched a shut out in Sulphur Dell received a watch from a local Jeweler. I can tell you that not too many watches were given away. The right field fence was about 270 feet away from home plate. Many times a pop fly that would have been caught for an out in other parks would end up a home run in the Dell.

It was an exciting park to play in. The right fielder stood on a path that was on a hill. There were times when a runner would be thrown out at first base on a one or two hop ball hit to the right fielder."

Al spoke about a Sunday when it was especially hot. He said, "There was an announcement made over the loud speaker informing the people that it was 107 degrees. My feet were really burning on that hot field," said Al. "Talk about heat, my spikes were hot to touch."

He continued on about the heat they were experiencing. "Our trailer had no air conditioning. It was like an oven inside it. Shirley's folks came down to visit us and all Dad Reusse could talk or think about was the cool weather back home in Minnesota. I like warm weather but when it gets so hot you can't enjoy it, it is too hot. I laid on the floor and hung my head out the door."

As Al thought about his entrance into professional baseball, there were numerous baseball men who touched his life, some more than others. Two men who were directly responsible for the big break were Dickey Martin and Larry Gilbert. Even when Al was not doing very well in the early part of the 1952 season, Larry Gilbert said, "I thought he was great when we signed him out of the University of Alabama just a year ago, but now I know he's better than ever as a major league prospect. He has two main essentials…a real live fastball and a curve that does something. He lacks nothing."

Between the end of the 1952 season and the spring training for the 1953 season, Al got a job working at Stockham Valve and Fitting in Birmingham. They pulled their trailer back to Birmingham from Nashville and set it up in a trailer park. The job at Stockham Valve and Fitting was tough and could be dangerous if one was not careful. Al said, "I worked from 4:30 p.m. to 1:00 a.m. One nice thing about the job was the benefit of a shower before I went home each night. I kept finding little slivers of steel in my legs. The work was hard. There was a saying among the people in the area that you haven't worked until you have worked at Stockhome.

I worked on a machine called the bullet. It cut iron or steel pieces down to a required size. The last night I worked there, I like to have lost a finger. That could have put an end to my baseball days."

17

SPRING TRAINING WITH THE GIANTS

"I was glad when it came time to go to spring training. I got an invitation to go to the New York Giants training camp to work out with them. They did not send me a plane or bus ticket. I was on my own but I didn't care too much. I was being invited to work out at a Major League training camp.

Shirley took Linda and went to stay with her parents in Minnesota. My mother made me a sack full of sandwiches and I took a bus to Phoenix, Arizona. It was a long ride by bus. I stopped and got off the bus in Tucson. Shirley had two aunts and an uncle who lived there.

We were eating Sunday dinner and I spotted brussels sprouts in a dish. They were passed to me and I passed them right on. Aunt Millie, without looking up, said, "Don't you like brussels sprouts?" I told her no. She said, "How do you know you don't like them?" That was a good question. I guess I knew I would not like them just by looking at them.

This was the first time I met these relatives of Shirley. They were super-nice to me. In fact, her aunt and uncle drove me to the Adams Hotel in Phoenix. I felt better about my situation with each passing day."

Al's first big league training camp was special for him. He was given $6.00 a day for meals. He believed he was with a good team. In 1951 they won the National League pennant. It was Bobby Thompson who struck the fatal blow. In fact, his game ending homerun was described as the shot that was heard around the world. During that 1953 spring training, he had the privilege of being with such players as Alvin Dark, Wes Westrum, Willie Mays, Monte Irvin, Bobby Thompson, Henry Thompson, Whitey Lockman, Don Mueller, Davy Williams, Sal Maglie, Jim Hearn, Larry Jensen, and others.

He finally got the opportunity to pitch against major league hitters. In exhibition baseball, the Giants played in what was called the cactus circuit. Al told of pitching against the Chicago Cubs in Mesa and the Cleveland Indians in Tucson. "I remember pitching three innings against Cleveland without giving up any runs. I think they got one hit off me."

Al was always trying to learn more about the game of baseball. He worked hard to develop the talent that God gave to him. He would be the first to tell you that all he wanted to do was do his best.

Something which Al did during that spring training and got into a habit of doing, was to go to the dog track which increased his desire to gamble. He said, "While in Phoenix, I went to the dog track. Since I already loved gambling, the dog track drew me like a magnet draws a nail to it.

It all started when I was a boy and played marbles for keeps. As I got older, I pitched quarters with the other fellows. The stakes got bigger. I was at the dog track nearly every night losing money that I didn't have to lose. I really was glad when I left Phoenix.

Before I leave this part of my story, I want to say that gambling never did me any good and it was one of the things, which was miraculously taken out of my life. Gambling owned me--it was in my blood. I could not stay away from it. Since God took it away from me 46 years ago I have not been tempted to start again. God can do the same for anyone who asks Him. He can take away the desire to gamble, smoke, drink and anything else that is holding him captive."

Spring training with the Giants was a wonderful opportunity for him and even if he didn't make the parent club then, he knew he eventually would be in the majors. He told Leo Durocher in the Phoenix training camp, "I did not come here expecting to make this team right off. I can not get an early start, but I know I can pitch, and I know I can make your team later on."

Durocher liked what he saw in the tall right-hander. In his own playing years, Leo Durocher was an aggressive determined player. He knew in his heart that he would be seeing the young man in a major league uniform in the future.

18

CONTRACT PURCHASED - MINNEAPOLIS BOUND

Another giant step was taken when Al was called into the office of Leo Durocher, the famed manager of the New York Giants. Leo, who was called 'The Lip', started out in professional baseball in 1925 with the New York Yankees. He later was part of the famous 'Gas House Gang' of the St. Louis Cardinals before going to the Brooklyn Dodgers where he later managed. Now, here he is managing the cross-town archrivals, the New York Giants. Alabama Al had little knowledge of the baseball background of the man who wanted to talk with him.

The stepping-stones became larger as the young man from Fulton Springs continued on his way. Wondering if he did anything right during his spring training with a roster filled with proven baseball stars or if he wasn't good enough to capture their attention, Al was nervous. After all, he was summoned to the office of the famous Leo Durocher for some reason which he was about to know.

Mom and Dad Worthington were unaware of the major decision that was about to be learned by their seventh child. Could the sweat on Al's face and arms be just from the Arizona heat or was it because Al was a bit scared as he stepped toward the office door of the man in charge of the New York Giants training base? He opened the door and walked into the office but not as a stranger. Al got to know him some during spring training. Durocher looked at Al and said, "We are buying your contract from Nashville and don't ask for any more money until you do something to earn it." Al shook the manager's baseball weathered hand and walked joyfully out of the offices.

"He gave me good advice," commented Al. "When I arrived in Phoenix, the Giants gave me my plane fare from Birmingham. From their Phoenix based training camp, they assigned me to the Minneapolis Millers, a triple A club, which was training in Melbourne, Florida.

Minneapolis was in the American Association, which is one step away from the major leagues. It gave me a wonderful feeling that I was no longer under a minor league contract. I was owned by the New York Giants."

Larry Gilbert was true to his word that Al would get one fourth of the sale of his purchase price. Al and Shirley smiled all the way to the bank to deposit the amount of $6,250.00 received from the New York Giants-Nashville Vols deal. Self-confidence was rapidly building within Al. His owner was the New York Giants.

The sports pages were ablaze with all kinds of information about Allan Fulton Worthington. In the Melbourne paper, The Sports section headline read, "Harshman dealt for Worthington." The Minneapolis Star carried comments from none other that Dick Reusse, Shirley's uncle and former baseball employer of Al when he played semi-pro ball.

Dick said, "Al pitched for us when we had one of the best teams in the state of Minnesota in 1950. We won 45 and lost 13.

He throws a fast ball that looks like a small aspirin when it comes across the plate...we hired him from the College World Series in Omaha. His first game was a one-hitter against Worthington, Minnesota and his no hitter was against Wilmot, also in Minnesota."

"A lump of cash and Jack Harshman" was the way one paper described the player transaction between the Giants and the Vols. Another sports writer said that, "Pitcher Al Worthington is a so-called 'stuff pitcher.' He may walk the bases full, then strike out the side." Still another baseball scribe said it this way. "Allan Worthington: Big Alabama University redhead, was 13 - 13 in 221 innings for Nashville last year and is tabbed by Frank Shellenback as a great prospect. Excellent "Stuff" but needs plenty of polishing." Leo Durocher was so amazed by Al's fastball that he said, "This big Al Worthington can throw hard. If he can throw enough strikes, he should win some."

As it is in the baseball profession, Al and Shirley were on the move again. He said, "They sent me to Florida to join the Minneapolis AAA Club. I met Shirley in Birmingham and we drove to Melbourne where Minneapolis was training. This was not new territory for us. How could we ever forget those delicious shrimp that we ate on a nearly daily basis?

Shirley, Linda and I lived in a cottage there until we broke camp that spring for the 1953 season. Chick Genovese was our manager. As I recall, I did not pitch for a week or more. I didn't mind one bit that I had not been pitching. The reason was that some of those early season night games were played in cold weather.

I finally started a game in Toledo, Ohio, against the Toledo Mud Hens. I felt pretty good on the mound that night. They only got six hits against our team's ten hits. I struck out twelve in twelve innings before being lifted in the thirteenth inning for pinch hitter, Chico Ibanez whose triple drove in two runs that were enough to win the game. That was my first win of the new season for Minneapolis."

107

Later on, the Toledo Mud Hens were playing the Millers on their home field at Nicollet Park. After shutting down a Toledo lineup that contained six left handed hitters with a strong wind blowing over the 280-foot right field fence, the Alabama hurler said, "I was lucky. I wasn't sharp."

"You mean to tell me," said George Selkiak, the Toledo manager, "that the big guy has only been pitching a year and a half? He's as rough as they come."

George Selkiak, who was known as Twinkle Toes, could speak with authority when it came to knowing baseball. He played in 846 games over a period of nine years for the New York Yankees. He also played in six World Series. Al had numerous good baseball men speak well of his pitching performance. Playing for the Minneapolis Millers in 1953 was a great experience for Al. He wanted, however, to clear up something. Even though he was told the Giants purchased his contract, he wanted to know if there were any ties with Minneapolis with whom he was playing, and Nashville from where he had come. He approached Rosy Ryan, the General Manager of Minneapolis, Al asked, "Who owns me, New York, Minneapolis or Nashville?"

"The Giants," answered Ryan."

"Thanks," said Al and nodded his head. "That's all I wanted to know."

The sportswriter who reported this conversation exchange in a Minneapolis paper said, "Worthington's potential is the greatest of any Miller twirler in history."

"Our manager, Chick Geneverse, was dismissed about halfway through the season," said Al. "He was replaced by Fred Fitzsimmons."

Fred Fitzsimmons or Fat Freddie as he was called, had a major league career of nineteen years. He spent thirteen years with the Giants and six years with Brooklyn. He had some good pitching years in baseball winning 217 and losing 146. With his wealth of experience he was a good man to work with Al.

"Shirley and I liked Minneapolis," Al commented one day talking about their latest home base. "We rented a house off 40th Avenue and enjoyed living there. When one moves as many times as we did in those few years, it wasn't too difficult to acclimate to new locations and neighbors.

It's hard for me to figure out some times how this baseball business is done," Al said one day. "I had a 13 - 13 season with Nashville, a second division club, which prompted the Giants to invite me to their 1953 Spring Training Camp. Now, here I am with Minneapolis on the doorstep to entering the major leagues. My goal is to do my best under any circumstance and let my abilities and accomplishments speak for me."

Playing with the Minneapolis Millers was a wonderful experience for the big guy from Fulton Springs, Alabama. He gave a lot of credit to the baseball men and their expertise that brought him to the level of ball played in the American Association. The previous year at Nashville with 221 innings pitched added greatly to the base of experience that was beginning to build for Al.

His efforts as a Miller quickly gained him the admiration of many not only in the state of Minnesota but also around the league. The start of the 1953 season was not what the newcomer would have chosen for himself. In 40 innings he gave up only five earned runs. One sports writer wrote, "Sometimes the Minneapolis Millers are going to get Al Worthington some runs and give their new pitching sensation an easy relaxing game to work. So far it's been nothing but pressure for the young right-hander." He pointed out that over the 40 innings the Millers gave Al only nine runs.

In a game with Columbus that was lost 3 – 0, Al struck out 10 and allowed only five hits in the first nine innings. His pitching prompted a sports writer to say, "It has been years since Nicollet Park has seen such blazing stuff as he cut loose."

Catcher Ray Noble asked Al one day, "Isn't there any way of letting me know which way those things are going to break?"

"Honest, Ray," replied Al, "I can't tell myself when I let that ball go."

One writer who kept a close eye on Al's baseball achievements said this about the promising pitcher, "A boy who is destined to stardom with the New York Giants, unless a great many experts who have watched his hopping fast ball are as cockeyed as the hitters who try to get a piece of it."

109

Bob Beebe of the Minneapolis Star wrote, "Add a large supply of pitching guts to a great assortment of hurling stuff and you have quite a pitcher—a real stopper. That's what the Millers have in young Al Worthington."

19

THE BIG TIME

The day finally arrived which Al had dreamed about and worked so hard to see come to pass. He said, "Word came from the Giants that they wanted me to join them. At the time, I had won nine and lost five for the Millers."

"Fred Fitzsimmons said that I was not ready for the majors. He thought I should finish out the season with Minneapolis and then go up to the big time. He probably was right."

When Al was called into the office at Nicollet Park to meet with Rosy Ryan and Fred Fitzsimmons, Shirley and little Linda waited in the anteroom. The attractive wife tried to keep from being nervous. Finally the door opened and the three men appeared. Looking at Ryan, she asked, "Is it what I think it is?"

When he said, "Yes," she burst into tears of joy. She said through the tears, "I'm so happy I can hardly talk."

Al's comment was, "I sure am surprised, I didn't expect it to come now after taking those whackings in the past couple of weeks. But it's what I've been aiming for-the Big Leagues. I want to say thanks for everything. Folks have treated me mighty fine around here."

The happy pitcher was not going to get away without some sound valuable advise from the two baseball scholars, Ryan and Fitzsimmons. "Remember," said the manager, "to do a lot of running when you get up there. I know you are in good shape but you've got to keep that way and you've got to show them you mean business. And don't forget to keep throwing overhand."

"Right," said Ryan. "You don't have your real good stuff when you don't come overhand. And your legs are as important as your arm. A pitcher starts losing it when his legs tire."

The young ball player listened intently as the two older men spoke to him. "One more thing," put in Fitz. "The ball is the same size up there and the bat's the same length. But they catch them a little better behind you."

"Once again, Mom and Dad Reusse came to our rescue as a family." Al said. "They did everything they could do to help Shirley in this latest move. Shirley went to live with them in Fulda."

There was much written and said about Al's promotion to the major leagues. Former infielder, Billy Johnson, who played six years with the New York Yankees and three years with the St. Louis Cardinals said, "Worthington is the only pitcher I have faced in the Association whose fast ball and curve moves...once he gains control, the boy should be a star up there."

Speaking of himself, Al said to reporters, "The only thing I've noticed is that my curve ball hasn't been breaking as well as I would like.

I could not help but wonder what Red Rolfe and Dixie Walker thought when they heard that I was called up by the Giants. And to think that I would have signed for nothing for Dixie's Atlanta Crackers just to play professional ball."

One sports writer wrote that Al knew where the platter was and the stuff he threw across it was a sight to behold. He went on to say that it was a long time since a Minneapolis Club had such an exhibition of powerhouse pitching as Al Worthington demonstrated.

Al got in on some of the story telling as well. He loved to tell the story when he was in his first year of professional ball with the Nashville Vols. He said, "I pitched a one hit game and didn't finish it. We led 1 – 0 into the ninth inning. I walked the first man and got the second batter out. I then walked the third man and got the fourth man out. Now there are two on and two out. I walked the fifth man loading the bases with still two out.

Don Osborn, the manager, took me out of the game. I was upset. Why, do you ask? Well, notice the rotation. It was my turn to get the next guy."

The writers referred to Al as a lot of things in order to describe his value to the Millers. One writer had this to say, "To say that Al Worthington has been worth a ton of gold to the Minneapolis baseball team this spring is putting it mildly."

Well, the 'ton of gold' was on his way to the famous Polo Grounds to play under the one and only Leo 'The Lip' Durocher.

"I flew to New York and got in about 11:00 p.m. There was no one to meet me. I went to the Henry Hudson Hotel, which was the Giants' hotel in New York. The next morning I was in the Giants' office at 9:00 a.m. They told me the team was next door on a train going to Philadelphia. Talk about me being confused! They said, "Go two doors down and go down the steps and catch the train there."

I walked out of the building as I was instructed to do but all I saw was cement and buildings wall-to-wall. There wasn't a train in sight and further more, I didn't see any train tracks. I finally walked past two doors and went down the steps. There were people walking about everywhere. I spotted a train. I never knew trains ran underground like that. I had never heard of a subway. I got on the subway and found my new manager, Leo Durocher. He greeted me by calling me Bill."

The young rookie exhibited a good attitude upon his joining the Giants. Being greeted as "Bill" by the manager who had observed his pitching at spring training camp and who personally told him of the purchase of his contract by the Giants, did not seem to bother Al at all. "It didn't matter to me what he called me. I was just happy to be among some of the best baseball players in the world. I figured Mr. Durocher would learn my name after I pitched a few times."

As previously mentioned, Al's outstanding performance in his first two major league assignments resulted with the establishment of a modern National League pitching record. "My first assignment was to pitch against the Philadelphia Phillies at home in the Polo Grounds. I shut them out 6 – 0 on two hits. Five days later, we went over to Brooklyn and played the Dodgers in Ebbets Field. I shut them out 6 – 0 on four singles.

My salary at that time was $5,000 for the year. Since it was already July when I entered the majors, half of the year was gone and so was half of my salary.

After Shirley arrived with Linda, we learned the subway system. We traveled from where our apartment was located to the Polo Grounds. I recall that the cost was ten cents per person. I thought that was pretty nice.

In fact, the most grass we saw that summer in New York City was in the Polo Grounds. That horse shoe shaped stadium made a real impression on us."

Al was given all kinds of advise on most everything he did playing baseball. A year before he joined the Giants, a veteran pitcher on the Nashville Club told him to kick the mound at times. He said that Al should look angry and pick up dirt and throw it down. Al said, "I followed his advice and did those things after a batter got a hit off me. Within a minute after I started acting that way, I began to feel really goofy. I knew I was doing something way out of character for me. I had followed bad advice. I learned that all advice is not necessarily good and especially when it goes against your character.

After my two shutouts in my first two games, Life magazine called my mother and asked if she had any pictures of me from babyhood on up. They wanted to print an article on me if I won my next game. I suppose they were thinking of a third consecutive shutout. My next game came eleven days later and it was against the Milwaukee Braves.

I felt I was in trouble because of the length of time since I last pitched. Even at that I lost to the braves by only a 2 – 1 score in a short five-inning game that made it official. With two out and a man on third base, the batter hit a ground ball, which went right through the shortstop's legs. We did not score and I received my first big league loss.

From there, everything seemed to go down hill. I finished the 1953 season with four wins and eight losses. Of course, I joined the Giants in the early part of July so I only had a half season with them. The last road trip was to Pittsburgh to play the Pirates; I took Shirley and Linda with me. We finished the season at Pittsburgh."

20

BASEBALL ACROSS THE PACIFIC

With the 1953 season ended for the Giants, Al took Shirley and Linda to Fulda where they would stay with Shirley's parents. The Giants were scheduled for exhibition games in Hawaii, Japan, Okinawa and the Philippines. He flew with the team to San Francisco where they stayed in the Fairmount Hotel. The next day they continued on to Honolulu. This was Al's first trip to any of these places.

An interesting thing about the trip was that Lorraine Day; the movie actress wife of manager Leo Durocher missed her birthday from Hawaii to Japan because of the International Date Line.

"The Japanese players made me a bit nervous," said Al. "They had very good eye sight and could see the ball well. I thought they were a bit slow in running. The umpires were very good. They, too, had sharp eyesight. They didn't miss many pitches, if any. The crowds were big but seemed very quiet. We could hear each other even from a distance."

Not all the Giant players made the trip. The ones who didn't go were Whitey Lockman, Alvin Dark, Sal Maglie, and Larry Jensen. The team took a train from Tokyo to Osaka where they played before a crowd of some 60,000. The team arrived late at the Okinawa airport. The baggage was slow coming to the pick-up place. One of the players made a remark loud enough for all to hear but actually directed it to the worker handling the baggage. The baggage handler heard the remark and looked up at the player. "You must be the umpire," he said. The remark made everyone laugh which eased any tension among the group.

"Our last two games of the trip were in Manila. We played a good Japanese team that had just defeated an American tour team that had all major league players on it. In one of the games I pitched, a Japanese player got two hits off me in two times at bat. The third time he came to bat, there were men on base. Leo Durocher came to the mound to talk to me. He said, "Don't walk the guy and don't give him anything good to hit." Leo's advice told me that Leo was never a pitcher. I knew I was not blessed with control and I think Leo knew that, too.

I thought of the tough situation I was in as Leo left the mound and walked back to the dugout. I tried to piece together the advice he gave to me but it didn't seem to fit. I was well aware that the short Japanese batter's strike zone was a small target for me. First of all, Leo said not to walk the guy. The second thing was that I was not to give him anything good to hit. I also knew that the umpires were very good at calling the pitches and if I were going to have any strikes called, I would have to get them within the strike zone.

I looked at the short batter crouched at the plate. "That sure is a small strike zone," I said to myself. I knew my teammates were rooting for me. I also knew that Leo was watching me like an eagle stares at its prey. A bad pitch could even possibly weaken

118

my chances of staying with the Giants. My catcher, Wes Westrum, held his mitt for my target. I threw the first pitch hard and fast straight down the middle. I wanted to overpower the Japanese batter. He swung the bat and happened to make contact with the ball and sent a ground ball to the shortstop. He fielded it cleanly and threw the batter out. It was a good pitch and a good play but we ended up losing the game 2 – 1. The Japanese pitcher, who pitched against us, had pitched against the American tour team the week before and won 2 – 1. I told our team that if we only scored one run, we will probably lose and we did.

It was fun playing those exhibition games. In one game we played the Central League All-Stars and won by a score of 7 – 0. There were 40,000 fans in Koshien Stadium, which seats between 70-90 thousand people. This is the largest stadium in Japan. I gave up three hits and even hit a double to help my cause."

On the exhibition tour, Al started five games and posted three wins. He said the Japanese fans love the game. The young people love baseball as well. Al mentioned that it was not unusual to see them out playing ball at 8 o'clock in the morning in large cities like Tokyo and Osaka.

Upon Al's return, a sports writer asked him what was his biggest thrill so far in baseball. Surprisingly, it was not his signing into pro ball or even his national league pitching record when he shut out the Phillies and Dodgers with 6 – 0 identical scores his first two games in the majors. He said, "My biggest thrill was the day I first stepped into the Polo Grounds. Boy! What a moment."

21

NOW WE ARE FOUR

Al headed for Fulda where Shirley and Linda were staying with Shirley's parents. He was anxious to do some duck and pheasant hunting. Talking about his hunting adventures, Al said, "I walked those corn fields many times and never got my limit of three. Now and then I got two but never three birds. It was like that in baseball sometimes. Getting that third out was tough."

Al and Shirley struggled at times to make ends meet financially. With the $6,250 which was the 25 percent paid to him by Nashville from the purchase price of his contract to the Giants, they bought the parsonage of the Methodist church where Al went as a boy. He said the price was around $6,000. Speaking of the house, Al said it was so solidly built that it would easily stand for

100 years or more. It was in Sunday school in the Methodist church where Al heard a clear statement by his Sunday school teacher about heaven and hell. She told the class, "There is a heaven and a hell. You are going to one of those places when you die." Al never forgot that statement as he got older. He remembers his boyhood friend, George Burris, being in the class with him. J.O. Richards, another close friend, went to a Baptist Church. The third of the quartet of friends, Cotton Crawford, went to the Church of Christ. Al said, "The four of us were always together when we were boys.

God allowed me to tell George Burris the story that Jesus suffered and died for him and that He paid for all of George's sin. He believed and invited Jesus to be his Savior. This took place in 1962. George became an outstanding churchman and Sunday school teacher. I spoke at my friend George's funeral around 1998."

With their own home in Alabama, Al, Shirley, and Linda left Fulda and went south. Shirley was the in late stages of her pregnancy with their second child. She woke up one morning at 3 o'clock and immediately woke up Al. She told him that the baby was coming. Al got up and, not having a telephone yet, drove down to his mother's house that was only a short distance away. After telling the doctor about Shirley's symptoms, he was told to tell her to go back to sleep. He went back home and both went back to sleep. The next time was no false alarm and on January 8, 1954, Allan made his appearance, increasing the Allan Worthington family to four.

22

TO PARENT CLUB AND WORLD SERIES

That spring Al joined the Giants in Phoenix, Arizona for Spring Training. Wanting him to have steady mound work, the Giants optioned him to the Minneapolis Millers on March 29. Al and Shirley liked the Minneapolis area. They had been there before and had made many friends. Baseball was their way of life and they learned to adjust themselves to the numerous changes they experienced.

Al said, "I think we played about two weeks on the road after the season opened. I did pretty well during the time I played for the Millers that year. I pitched in 24 games completing ten of them. I won eleven and lost seven. In the 152 innings that I pitched, I had 93 strikeouts. On July 27, word came from the Giants that I was to report to them. This time I did not want to go. Most players would have jumped at the chance of going to the majors. I was having a good year with Minneapolis and I wanted to finish the season with the club. I went to Rosy Ryan, the General Manager, and told him that I did not want to go. I said, "Let me stay here and pitch the rest of the season and I will go up next year."

Al made it very clear what his desire was as far as moving up to the Giants. He enjoyed pitching for the Millers. In fact, he said, "I liked Minneapolis. Playing ball in the minor leagues was fun for me." He then added that he had no choice. He had to go. He always talked things over with Shirley who wanted the best for her husband.

From the start of the 1954 season to the time of his recall on July 27 there was continuous praise for the big 6' 2" pitcher from Alabama from the baseball scribes as well as from his teammates.

Bob Beebe, a Minneapolis Star staff writer wrote, "It's May, so Worthington Blooms." Another writer said the following about Al during the early part of the 1954 Millers' season; "Al Worthington is a major league pitcher right now, when his arm ailment is under control. Keep that kink subdued and nothing can hold him out of the majors." After pitching against the Kansas City Blues and the Indianapolis Indians, one of the sports writers said, "On those two efforts alone, Worthington must be rated as the best pitching prospect in the Giants' minor league chain."

Al's departure for the parent club deprived him the privilege of appearing in the American Association All-Star game in Indianapolis. He led the Upper Midwest balloting with 5,010 votes edging out such star players as Rocky Colovito with 4,960 and Herb Score with 4,630.

To make room for Al on the Giants roster, Ramon Monzant was sent back to Minneapolis. He had been called up to the Giants from Minneapolis on June 27, so was only with the parent club for a month. Al was flying out of the Minneapolis Airport for New York the same time that Monzant was arriving from New York.

Regarding his return to the Giants, Al said, "I know I'm more ready to pitch in the National League this year than I was when I

124

went up last season." It was not going to be all new names and faces for Al to learn this time. In fact, among his teammates were the two fellow pitchers with whom he rode over to Brooklyn the previous year when he set a modern major league pitching record. Jim Hearn and Sal Maglie were there to greet him.

The Giants were in the pennant race and eventually won the pennant, Al was not the help he thought he would be to the team. When the regular season ended, he had appeared in ten games and had no wins and two losses. Al was miserable. "It's not fun when you do not play good consistently."

He was quick to say that he was not miserable with the game. "Baseball is by far the greatest game to play," he said.

"There is no other game that is even a close second. At best, that's my thinking." As bad as he felt about his poor contribution to the team, he felt good in being a part of the Giants and being in the World Series.

The Cleveland Indians won the American League pennant. Al purchased a number of tickets for the series. Shirley, Linda and Allan, arrived at Kennedy International Airport where Al met them.

Going to the airport he rode to the end of the subway line then caught a bus to the airport from there. The family of four took a cab to go to Al's apartment in the Concourse Plaza that was near Yankee Stadium. He said the cab ride cost $5. He felt pretty good about paying a total of only twenty cents to go to the airport by subway and bus.

There was disappointment in Al when no one from Birmingham called him for tickets. He did say, "I had two tickets for mama and pop who took their first plane trip to get to New York. It made me feel so good to have my parents there with us.

When the Cleveland Indians showed up at the Polo Grounds, their hard-hitting third basemen, Al Rosen, had a leg injury that hampered his running. We all knew what such an injury could do to the Indians chances of winning the series.

Dusty Rhodes won the first game for us with a pinch-hit home run. We also took the second game giving us a big advantage point as we moved on to Cleveland's huge Municipal Stadium to continue the series. By this time, the adrenalin was really flowing.

It really did not matter much to us that we were playing a team that just won 112 games setting a new major league record for games won in a 154 game schedule.

Even though I didn't play in the series, I had one of the best seats to watch the games. Being on the Giants' bench was like having a ringside seat at a boxing match or sitting on the 50-yard line at a football game. I was privileged to see one of the greatest catches in baseball when Willie Mays made that sensational catch of the ball that Vic Wertz hit to deep center field at the Polo Grounds."

The Giants took the first two games at Cleveland giving them the series in four games. All four games were well attended with packed houses in both New York and Cleveland with capacity seating of 50,000 and 80,000.

When it came to dividing up the World Series shares, Al thought the team did well by him for the short time that he was with the Giants. They voted him one-third share, which amounted to $3,000. He said, "That was very generous of them for what little I contributed to the team. Then, too, I had an exceptionally good seat for the four games."

When the team arrived back in New York from Cleveland, the president of the Giants, Horace C. Stoneham, hosted a party for the World Series winners. One of the things that Al remembers well was the huge stack of raw oysters for everyone to help himself. Al felt out of place at the party. He describes his feeling by saying, "The other players deserved to be there but not me. I did not really feel right about being there. I was 0 – 2 for the season and did not play in the World Series."

One of the events, which caused a smile to spread across Al's face, was his participation along with his teammates and Giants officials in the ticker-tape parade down Wall Street. Riding in an open car surrounded by tens of thousands of people raised goose pimples on Al.

"It was like a big snow storm, only it was pieces of paper coming from the business offices above. I had never experienced anything like that."

23

BACK TO THE MILLERS

The winter seemed to pass rather quickly for Al and Shirley.
Many who knew Al liked to talk with him about baseball. He
didn't mind even going back a year or more to talk about things
that happened. One of those times was on September 10, 1953, in
St Louis. Leo Durocher chose Al to pitch against the Cardinals.
The 24 year-old youngster, as many called him, lost to St Louis by
a score of 7 - 6. "Had it not been for two infield errors in the
eighth inning," one sports writer said, "Worthington probably
would have won the game."

"He got that big out and that's what counts," said a friend of
the promising young pitcher. He was referring to what would be a
dream for most pitchers. The Cards managed to get at least one
man on base every inning. In the fourth inning, Al retired Stan
(The Man) Musial with the bases loaded. Manager Leo Durocher

was very pleased with that outstanding feat of young Al. One sports writer said, "It's been a long time since Durocher has seen one of his pitchers get Musial out in a tough situation."

It was time to leave for Phoenix and 1955 spring training. Times had changed drastically for Al. He didn't like to think about the struggle he had trying to get the attention of a minor or major league ball club. Having been in professional baseball, even on the major league level, he knew there would be a place somewhere for him.

When the Giants left Phoenix for a three game series in the Los Angeles, Al was left behind. Regarding that decision by Leo Durocher, he said, "That should have told me something." The only other person left behind was Ronnie Samford and he had been sold or traded to the Detroit Tigers.

"I was still addicted to gambling at the dog tracks," recalled Al. "I was there every night losing my money. I can tell you that I definitely was not a good example for any one and especially many young people who look to sports figures to be examples for them. For things I did which were not good examples, I look upon them with shame."

The expected news came. Al received word on April 2, 1955, that he was optioned to Minneapolis of the American Association. He said, "I was to report to the Millers' training camp in Sanford, Florida. To be honest about it, I really was glad to go. The Giants officials didn't think I could help them at that time and sent me to Minneapolis where they thought I could be a help."

Bill Rigney, the playing manager of the Millers, was in his second year. He gave Al the opening season assignment against the Indianapolis Indians. The man from Alabama was so concerned about his opening night assignment that he sang while getting his pre-game arm rub from trainer, Tommy McKenna. The trainer said that Al didn't sing like the eminent baritone and chef, Ralph Branca, but his vocal efforts reflected his mood and that of the Millers who went on to blank Indianapolis 5 – 0 behind the four hit pitching of Al.

Even though the season had just started, there was that feeling among the players that they were a solid unit which could go all the way including winning the Little World Series. "We all had a lot of confidence," said Al. A pitcher needs good battery-mates and I had them. Carl Sawatski was especially capable behind the plate as well as being a powerful hitter. Ray Dabek was a good back up for Carl."

24

A FANTASTIC FINISH

The 1955 season was a fantastic year for the Millers. Al had his best season since he entered professional ball. He pitched in 38 games, tied for the lead with 33 starts, led the league in complete games with 18, led the league with 19 wins against 10 losses, struck out 150 and had an earned run average of 3.58.

The Millers swept the American Association playoffs winning over Denver and Omaha in an unprecedented eight straight games to go into the Junior World Series with the Rochester Red Wings of the International League. One of the baseball scribes wrote, "As long as the Minneapolis Millers can keep Al Worthington's pitching arm healthy, they are going to do all right in any post season baseball meetings." He certainly was to be a prophet in his prediction.

Al was concerned in the last playoff game with the Omaha Cardinals when his number one battery-mate Carl Sawatski, was injured. The Miller catcher was hit on the back of his head by Danny Schell's missed follow through swing. Carl went down bleeding badly but got up and walked to the clubhouse. He was taken to an Omaha hospital where he received three stitches to close the wound. He was back in harness to open the Junior World Series with Rochester.

The seven game series with the Red Wings was a fight to the finish. Al appeared in four of the seven games and won three of them. This tied a record held by seven others with the most wins in the Junior World Series. Al, with 19 wins for the season, said after the seventh and final game, "I didn't want the win. I was glad Floyd (Melliere) got it."

Manager Bill Rigney credited the whole homer-hitting Millers squad but "without Worthington we wouldn't have been close enough in a lot of games to pull out the win in the later innings with home runs. Whatta pitcher! He'll pitch for me with the Giants next season."

In the clubhouse after the game, Dixie Walker, the losing Rochester manager, paid his respect to the champion Millers. In his remarks he said, "And that Worthington – he can pitch in the majors." Just a few years before, the same Dixie Walker, when managing the Atlanta Crackers, refused to allow Al to even pitch batting practice.

One of the interesting things about the Junior World Series was the difference in baseballs. He said, "I think they used the Spalding-made ball in the International League. We used the Wilson-made ball in the American Association. The Spalding ball was too big for my hand. In fact, I threw about three wild pitches with that ball and my control was not good."

Things are often said on the playing field among players that the fans don't hear," said Al. "For example, we were losing to Rochester 3 – 2 in the seventh inning of game six. A win by the Red Wings would have ended the series right then. As we were taking the field in the top of the seventh, George Wilson, our right fielder hit me on the rump with his glove as he went by." He said,

"Hold them, Red, I'm coming up our next at bat." I held them and when George came to bat, he tied the score with a homerun.

Neither team scored in the eighth or ninth innings. As we were taking the field in the tenth inning, George passed by me again and said, "Hold them again, Red, it's my turn to bat this inning." Once again Al kept the Red Wings from scoring in their half of the inning. In the bottom of the tenth, George came to bat and promptly hit one out of the park to win the game for the Millers.

Bill Rigney was named Minor League Manager of 1955. He had already signed a contract to succeed Leo Durocher as manager of the New York Giants for 1956. Rigney said at the close of the season that one of his pitchers for the Giants would be Al Worthington. He had great respect for Al's pitching ability. In talking about the Millers' great '55 season, he said, "I'll never forget what he (Al Worthington) did for me."

The baseball season was a fun time but a very busy one. "It left me tired," said Al. "I had pitched 239 innings for the Millers but for some reason, I was ready to start pitching in the Puerto Rican League. Shirley, too, was extremely tired. She would get up with baby Allan at 4 a.m. and always waited up for me until I got home, usually after 11 p.m. The doctor told her she needed a rest."

25

PUERTO RICO

"We arrived in Puerto Rico and were pleased with our nice furnished apartment on the sixth floor. Across the street was a hotel that had beautiful grounds. There was a nice place where we could buy hamburgers, soda pop, ice cream, etc. We also had a pool and a volleyball court. We swam in the ocean but mostly in the pool. It cost $35 a month to be members of the hotel club. In just two weeks time, we were ready to return home. I felt terrible. I went to a doctor to see if I had something wrong with me. When he asked me if I wanted to be there, I told him 'no'. He prescribed burnt toast for me to eat. He said it would do me good by cleaning out my system. After many years, I still eat burnt toast if I am not feeling well. That doctor never realized how long that prescribed treatment would last."

Al pitched the season's opener for Santurce against Caguas-Guayama and shut them out, 6 – 0 with a one-hit gem. He won nine games in a row for Santurce. He said, "I was paid $1,000 a month and got $350 in addition for living expenses. I still was addicted to gambling and returned home to Alabama broke.

We could have had such a wonderful time as a family in Puerto Rico," Al said, "But I allowed gambling to enslave me. I felt guilty and helpless because of that terrible habit. I knew about God and actually prayed to Him for help. He seemed like someone far away. I knew that I really needed Him but I didn't know how to find Him."

26

NO RECALL – NO OPTION

Another spring training camp was ready to begin. Al did not have to worry about a job. Bill Rigney had already named him as part of his Giants pitching staff for 1956. As much baseball as Al had played since he signed with Nashville in 1951, the 1955 season with Minneapolis was definitely his best year up to that time. His 19 wins were the most he had recorded in his five years of ball. Then, too, he and Bill Rigney were named the outstanding manager and athlete of the year in the State of Minnesota. In fact, no one else came close in the United Press poll of newspaper sports editors, television and radio sportscasters throughout the State.

At a press conference, Bill Rigney, discussed his plans for the Giants in '56. He said, "I would like to go with young new players if I can. I have several newcomers in mind that I think have a good chance to make it. One is Allan Worthington, who did a wonderful job for me in Minnesota."

With the National League season underway, Al won his first game since the final week of the 1953 season. For his part in the 5 – 3 win over Philadelphia, Al said, "I started off pretty shaky at first but once I settled down, I was all right. They only got six hits off me and I helped my own cause by bringing in a run in the second inning with a sacrifice fly. I was very pleased with my nine strikeouts."

"During the '56 season," said Al, "we lived in a house in Yonkers, New York. We paid $200 a month. Shirley and I liked it there. In fact, I think that I would have liked it even more had my pitching record been better. My seven wins against 14 losses didn't make me feel too good. I did, however, appear in 28 games, pitched 166 innings and struck out 95. A real accomplishment is that we learned how to drive in New York."

Carl Hubbell, who pitched for the Giants for 16 years and who was voted into the Hall of Fame in 1947, was very high on Al. The Giants' farm boss hoped that Al might possibly replace Sal Maglie who had been the Giants' lead right-hander against the Flock from Flatbush Avenue across town. He said about Al, "He has the equipment to pitch well against the Dodgers. He could be the lead pitcher against them, which is, of course, what we need."

Bill Rigney, in adding his praise for "Red" as he called Al now and then, said this, "Work? The guy's got to work. I rested him five days for an important game. He didn't last an inning. He has to pitch steady. He would pitch every other day if I'd let him."

The 1956 season ended without much fanfare, although Al did have a close call in a game with Pittsburgh. It was the sixth inning with the Pirates' first baseman, Dale Long, at the plate. Long, a hard hitter, lined one back at Al striking him on his left forearm. A huge welt rose up immediately. X-rays showed there was no bone broken. Had the ball hit just a bit lower the wrist could have been hurt badly.

"We played our last game of the '56 season with the Phillies," said Al. "Rigney wanted to see some of his younger pitchers work but for some reason he chose me to pitch against the Phillies' future Hall of Fame pitcher, Robin Roberts. Robin was looking for his 20th win of the season and if he was going to get it, he had to be the winner of the game."

The Giants won the game 8 – 3 with Al hitting his one and only home run in the majors. He said, "I didn't claim to be even a good hitter. Facing a great pitcher like Robin Roberts, I felt like I was out before I even got to the batter's box. Well anyway, Robin threw what I call a fat pitch. I swung and made contact with the ball and drove it toward the stands in left field. I could hardly believe it when it landed in the seats. I had a total of 12 hits that summer but that home run was the greatest hit of them all.

I knew somewhat how Robin felt when I hit the home run against him. During my few years in baseball up to that time; I had my share of home runs hit off me."

Manager Rigney was talking to Robin Roberts later on. The famous pitcher said to the Giants' Manager, "I am glad you pitched Worthington against me. If you had worked a youngster and I had won, some wise guys would have said that I had a setup just so I could win number 20. As much as I wanted it, I am glad it worked out the way it did."

Rigney couldn't get over what Roberts told him. "There's a right guy," he commented. "No wonder he is such a great pitcher."

27

WELCOME MICHELE – GOODBYE POLO GROUNDS

The year, 1957, brought with it even greater challenges. Al said, "We had moved from Yonkers, a borough of New York City, to a town in Northern New Jersey called River Edge. It was only a short distance from New York City. We rented a nice big house for $150 a month.

Shirley was in her third pregnancy and was getting close to the date the doctor told us the baby would be born. On July 21, 1957, she showed signs that the birth of the baby was approaching. Neither Shirley nor I expected the baby to arrive immediately. The wife of one of my teammates offered to keep Linda and Allan while I took Shirley to the hospital in Teaneck, a nearby town. I took her to the hospital and went on from there to the Polo Grounds because we had a game that night."

Al got to the ballpark and got dressed for the game. While the game was in progress, word arrived from the hospital that Shirley had given birth to a baby girl. The large Polo Grounds crowd cheered loudly as the good news of baby Michele's birth was flashed on the huge scoreboard. Needless to say, Al could hardly wait to get back to the hospital in Teaneck to be with Shirley and the newest arrival in the Worthington family. Shirley's parents in Fulda, Minnesota, heard the news on the radio and caught a plane so they could be with Al and Shirley and the three grandchildren. They now represented three states. Linda was born in Worthington, Minnesota. Allan was born in Birmingham, Alabama, and Michele was born in Teaneck, New Jersey.

The '57 baseball season was a bit of a disappointment to Al only because he thought he didn't do enough for the team. He did appear in 55 games. That was 27 more than the year before. His eight wins and eleven losses was an improvement for him over the year before when he had seven wins and fourteen losses. His pitching ability produced 90 strikeouts for the year.

The close of the '57 season also brought an end to the Giants team in New York City. Coogan's Bluff, or Hollow, as some called it became the location of the Polo Grounds in 1889. After numerous additions and changes, it finally ended up with a seating capacity of 56,000.

It served over the years as the home of the Giants, New York Yankees, and New York Mets. Many monumental happenings took place at the Polo Grounds. Willie May's unbelievable over the shoulder catch of Vic Wertz's drive into deep center field was one that Al witnessed. The famous Hall of Fame playing manager, Mel Ott, hit 323 of his 511 home runs there. The Giants' last game at the Polo Grounds was with the Pittsburgh Pirates on September 29, 1957. They lost to the Pirates 9 – 1.

29

EXCITING SAN FRANCISCO

The year of 1958 was a year that would change the lives of Al and Shirley Worthington forever. The time to leave for spring training came and it was off to Phoenix again. "I told Shirley," said Al, "this will be the year that I will find the peace that I have looked for."

This time after spring training, it would not be back east and the Polo Grounds. Instead, it would be starting the season in Seals Stadium that was the home park of the San Francisco Seals, a team in the Triple A Pacific Coast League.

The Brooklyn Dodgers, as well, went to the West Coast the same year and made their home in Los Angeles. Both teams changed their names with the Giants becoming the San Francisco Giants and the Dodgers renamed the Los Angeles Dodgers. The two former cross-town archrivals were still close but this time in different California cities. The Giants would eventually play two years at Seal Stadium before moving to their new stadium, Pacific Ball Park.

New surroundings usually did not excite Al and Shirley that much. They both loved the game of baseball but the constant travel and continuous moving began to wear thin. Then, too, they always seemed to have that empty feeling that something very important was missing in their lives. For example, in Phoenix, Shirley who was a Roman Catholic asked a priest where purgatory was found in the Bible. She said, "I married a Protestant and he wanted to know where purgatory is found in the Bible."

He looked at her and said, "That is just like a Protestant. You have to prove everything to them." Shirley was not impressed at all with his answer.

The hunger for something to satisfy that emptiness in their lives was out there somewhere but they could not identify just exactly what it was or how it could be found.

The years that Al spent in New York were not enjoyable years for him. In fact, he would say to the clubhouse manager, Eddie Logan, "I am not coming back, Eddie." The good natured Eddie would laugh and say, "I'll see you in the spring." Pointing to all his equipment that he was taking home with him, Al would respond, "You will not see me again." Eddie seemed to know Al better than Al knew himself because he would show up in the spring.

Trying to describe his feeling, Al said, "I was tired of leaving home and going on road trips, living in hotels, and going to baseball parks. The biggest thing was the emptiness that was inside me. I knew it was an emptiness that I could not fill. I laughed like I had peace within me but to be honest; there was no true peace. The years of sports that I played did not give me the peace that I so much wanted.

Ever since my Sunday school teacher said there is a heaven and hell and that I would go to one of those places, I started my search for heaven when I was about eleven years old."

San Francisco is an exciting place. The man from Fulton Springs, Alabama said, "San Francisco was the most exciting place

I had ever been. The people were great to us. Big league baseball had come to California and the people were excited. I remember the song, 'San Francisco,' was played on the radio a lot during the day. At times I thought that San Francisco must be the most beautiful place on earth.

I could sit and look at the Golden Gate Bridge. Just seeing it fascinated me. The quaint houses with the Spanish architecture captivated me. The famous trolley car was fun to ride and Fishermen's Wharf was interesting to visit. Shirley and I tried to enjoy to the fullest the area's sights."

Playing in Seal Stadium was a privilege to Al. He said, "I think of the many Seal players who went on to stardom in the Major Leagues. One of the greatest of that group of former Seals was Joe DiMaggio who played thirteen years for the New York Yankees. Joe set a Major League record of hitting in 56 consecutive games. While playing for the Seals, he hit safely in 61 straight games. Joe was one of the three DiMaggio brothers who played in the Major Leagues at the same time. The other two were Vincent (Vince), and Dominic (Dom) who was also known as the Little Professor. All three brothers had the name of Paul for their middle name.

Even though Al was disappointed in his pitching performance, he definitely was holding his own compared to the previous season. They rented a house in Redwood City that was twenty-five miles south of San Francisco. "It was a beautiful location to live," commented Al. "The house was owned by another pitcher, Don Mossi, who was playing at the time for Cleveland and who went to Detroit the following year. It was exciting to both Shirley and me to live in that beautiful area in such a comfortable house."

Al rode to the park with Daryl Spencer and Paul Giel in Paul's convertible with the top down in 90-degree weather.

Al was amused as he told about his next-door neighbor. He said, "I just loved to walk out and enjoy that southern California sun. My next-door neighbor was outside a lot as well. I would say, "Beautiful day, isn't it?" His response was always the same just like my comments were the same. His pat answer was, "Every day is beautiful out here." For some reason that struck Al as being funny, "It's strange what things people remember," said Al.

Thoughts about God and heaven and what his Sunday school teacher said stayed with Al. A man by the name of Marshall DeVaughn came to Al one day and asked if he and teammate Bob Speake would serve on a committee for a softball league.

"I was always ready to help people," said Al, "and I figured that it would be a good distraction and be fun to do. Bob was very interested and wanted to be involved. I suppose his enthusiasm attracted me even more than to help Marshall DeVaughn. I was introduced to two other men who were friends of Marshall DeVaughn. One was Bill Austin and the other was Don Jones. They were both preachers. When I found out that they were from the east, I asked them what they were doing out in California. All three gave me the same answer, they said, "God sent me out here."

"After hearing what they said, I asked myself, "Why didn't God send me out here?" I had no idea what the men were talking about. Without realizing what was happening, the softball committee subject seemed to fade out of the picture.

29

THE COW PALACE

Unknown to Al, the Billy Graham Crusade team was holding meetings in the famous Cow Palace in San Francisco. Bob Speake approached Al and said, "Hey Al, Joan and I are going to hear Billy Graham preach at the Cow Palace. Would you and Shirley like to go with us?"

"What is he going to preach about," Al asked his teammate.

"Whatever he says, it will be good," responded Bob, "Come on and go with us. You'll be glad you did."

When they walked into the Cow Palace, they could hardly believe what they saw. The place was packed with thousands of people. They made their way onto the main floor area and sat down. The crowd sang like they meant it. When Billy Graham started preaching, the eyes of the people were glued on him as they took in every word.

"I heard him but I did not understand what he was talking about," said Al. "When he got through preaching, he then invited the people to accept Christ as their Savior. Again, I didn't know what he meant. I thought I must be the best person there because I never killed anybody or stole anything except watermelons back in Georgia when I went to play baseball.

After the meeting was over, Shirley and I met with Marshall DeVaughn along with Bob and Joan Speake and went to the DeVaughn's house. There Marshall told us that he was a recruiter for Christ. I didn't understand that kind of terminology. He proceeded to tell us about God and how He delivered him from a life of sin.

As Shirley and I sat there and listened to Marshall pour out his heart about God's greatness and all that He meant to him, I wondered if God could do that for Shirley and me as well."

Al and Shirley met with Marshall three days in a row. Every question they could think of to ask him, he was quick to answer directly from the Bible. There was one thing that was bothering Al so he asked Marshall about it.

"How come," said Al, "that Billy Graham lives in such a nice house and dresses in nice clothes?"

Marshall hesitated a moment and then looked at Al. He said, "Would you like for him to live in the woods and wear animal skins for clothes? Who would listen to him if he lived and dressed like that?"

"You're right," responded Al. "I understand now. I really do understand."

Al and Shirley went back to the Cow Palace to hear Billy Graham preach. Again, the place was packed with people. They had to go to the top balcony where they sat in the aisle on a concrete step. When the well-known evangelist finished his sermon, he proceeded to give an invitation and the large choir began to sing.

"Just as I am without one plea,
But that Thy blood, was shed for me.

148

And that Thou bid'st me come to thee,
Oh, Lamb of God, I come, I come."

Al knew something inside was happening to him. He said, "My heart began to pound so hard, I spread my hands on my chest to keep it from being heard. Never had it beat so hard before. Since the last time we were at the Cow Palace, I had been asking God to give me the desire and help me to know Him.

I knew just being there at the Crusade was not enough. At the same time, I wondered why my heart was pounding so hard. It seemed my mind was racing beyond control. God was answering my prayers and I didn't realize it. I thought of the time I had been baptized and joined the church. I thought of the eighth grade Sunday school class I once taught. Were these things that God wanted me to be doing to please him? I felt at times I was giving God 50, 60 and even 70 percent of my efforts but I knew there was more to it than that. When did I ever go to Jesus as Billy Graham was saying? I honestly did not know if I really ever went to Jesus in the way the preacher described it.

In my heart, I was bending my knees to God. I told Shirley that I had to go forward. I just could not stay there and resist the tremendous pull on my heart. I finally started down to the main floor where a crowd was gathering by the hundreds. I decided to give God my life and surrender my all to Him. I would call Him Lord. I was determined that I would give him 100 percent. I would be His servant and He would be my God. I did not care who saw me walking down from the balcony.

I did not know one Bible verse by heart. The thought came to mind, what about the fellows on the team? What will they think when they hear about what I have done? It really didn't matter what they or anyone else thought. It was something I had to do. I was not in charge of my life anymore. I thought whatever happens is totally up to God."

Al went forward, Shirley also went down to the main floor. God had been working in her heart long before spring training. She said, "I simply went all alone and was scared." Shirley knew she had to make a decision. Al was taken into a room where a man talked and prayed with him. He was given literature to help him.

When he came out, Shirley was waiting for him. Over one thousand others left their seats and gathered on the main floor. As far as Al was concerned, he made the decision to give his all to the Lord and there was no turning back.

"One Bible verse that explains many things to me and one of my favorites is found in Jeremiah 29:13, It reads, "And ye shall seek me, and find me, when ye shall search for me with all your heart." I had looked for God for years but had never really searched with all my heart." Explained Al, "That night I came calling on God."

Al saw people crying and didn't understand why they were doing it. For him, it was a commitment to give God his life. He said, "God, I have come to tell you that I want to live for you the best I know how. I don't know much about what is taking place right now but I want to give you my all."

Al held tightly onto the literature that was given to him. When he and Shirley left the Cow Palace, they went to the DeVaughn's house. Brother DeVaughn was not home yet because he was taking two young people home who had been to the meeting. After a short time, Brother DeVaughn arrived. When he walked into the house, his wife said to him, "Al gave his life to the Lord tonight." Her husband walked over to Al and said, "Al, I've been praying for you."

"I was surprised to hear what he said to me," Al recalled. "I thought, why are you praying for me? What have I done wrong? Why are you so glad? On the way home that night, I knew something was happening to me that was far beyond my control."

The next day the Giants left on a road trip for seventeen days. Al said, "I hated to leave Shirley and the children. In fact, I counted the days and hours until I would get back home. I could not get over the way I felt."

150

30

NEW CREATIONS

Looking back to that time, the things that were taking place in Al's life reminded him of the wonderful verse in II Corinthians 5:17 which he didn't know at the time was in the Bible. The verse reads, "Therefore if any man be in Christ, he is a new Creature: old things are passed away; behold all things are become new." Al said even his worries were gone. "In fact," he said, "I sat down three times and tried to worry about the usual things that worried me. All three times I jumped up filled with joy instead of worries. It seemed like my former worries were put on a high shelf that I could not reach."

At the airport, one of the players was standing outside the plane. He said, "Al, let's play cards." I looked at him and said,

"No, I won't be playing cards. I want to find out more about what is happening to me."

On the flight to Pittsburgh, Al said the Lord seemed very close to him. The more he thought about his heart pounding experience under Billy Graham's preaching, the more he marveled at the changes taking place in his life. "During the flight I read my Bible and for the first time, I knew Jesus was speaking to me. I never understood the Bible before. I don't want you to think I had never read the Bible before. Each Spring I would put my Bible in my suitcase on my way to spring training. I would say, Lord, just in case the airplane falls, You know I'm on Your side." Al just could not understand what was happening in his heart. He said, "I knew it was God."

The team arrived in the Steel City and went to their hotel. Word spread fast among the team that "Al was getting religion." The man from Alabama still could not fully understand why he felt the way he did. He knew that God was doing it but what all was He doing? He was giving him love, joy and His peace.

The next morning he never felt so good in all his life. Within his heart, he had perfect peace. He opened his Bible and read in Psalms 37:4, "Delight thyself also in the Lord; and He shall give thee the desires of thine heart."

As the Holy Spirit ministered to Al through the Word, he knew that he trusted Christ as his Savior. He read that his body was the temple of the Holy Spirit. He read that he was born again. The new believer could hardly control his emotions. What started at the Cow Palace came into fruition. Allan Fulton Worthington was a new creation in Christ. He knew that he just could not keep it to himself what God had done for him.

He called Shirley and told her not to worry about him. He said, "If the plane goes down on this road trip, I'm going up."

"Man searches for love, peace, fame, and riches. These things, however, can only be found in Jesus Christ. I went down to the dining room and ordered my breakfast. Later, I went to pay my bill. I just had to tell the young lady cashier that I was saved. She listened very carefully to every word. Her eyes were focused on me and her mouth seemed to open with awe at what she was hearing. I really thought that I might have sounded a bit crazy telling her what I did. The message was on my heart and I felt compelled to tell it.

The next day, after the game, about seven of us ate at the hotel around a big table. When the waitress asked me what I wanted to drink, I said nothing. A veteran ballplayer at the other end of the table said, "Why aren't you having a drink?" I said, "I don't want one." He responded, "Why don't you want one?" By that time, I was really scared. I don't see how anyone could be more scared than I was sitting there in front of my teammates.

Finally, I said to him, "The other night at the Billy Graham Crusade, I accepted Jesus Christ as my Lord and Savior and I do not know if He wants me to drink or not, and until I find out, I won't be having a drink." There was complete silence at the table. To this day, God has never told me that I can drink.

At age 29, I had never heard a man confess Jesus Christ as his Lord and Savior. I then went upstairs to my room and opened my Bible. God said if you are hungry, I will feed you and if you are thirsty, I will give you drink. I prayed, "Oh, God, I am thirsty for Your Word and I am hungry for Your Word." Power from heaven came upon me. I believe it was because I confessed Him at the table." Al was growing by leaps and bounds in his newfound faith.

While they were still in Pittsburgh, Al said, "I was on my way to the stadium for our game, when all of a sudden, I reached into my pocket and pulled out my pack of cigarettes and handed them to a friend who was with me. He said, "What are you doing?" I answered, "God doesn't want me to smoke anymore." I thought how could I tell him that, when I had stopped smoking and started again many times. I knew it sounded good to me what I had said to him but did I have the strength to stop for good? I knew the Lord would give me the victory."

The Giants finished their series with the Pirates and went on to Philadelphia. Al knew he needed the Lord's help if he was to kick his old habits. He took his Bible and opened it to I Corinthians 10:13 where he read, "There hath no temptation taken you but such as is common to man: but God is faithful, who will not suffer you to be tempted above that ye are able: but will with the temptation also make a way to escape, that ye may be able to bear it."

"When I read the verse, I immediately thought that God had put that verse in the Bible especially for me. I was craving for a cigarette. I left the room and returned two hours later. The craving to smoke was still there. I opened my Bible to I Corinthians 10:13 and read it over and over again. Since that time, I have not put a cigarette to my mouth. God kept His Word."

Being a Christian changed many things in Al's life. He said that while pitching for the Giants, it was customary that when a pitcher won a game, he would buy a beer for each of the other pitchers on the team. Al told them, "I can't buy you a beer but I will buy you a sandwich." He said when he won; he didn't have to buy any sandwiches! I ended that tradition.

The Bible became very precious to Al. It became his number one past time. It seemed every spare moment he had, he would get his Bible out and read it. He would often say, "Lord, I'm not smart enough to understand Your Word, please help me."

Another habit that Al had was to bite his fingernails. He did that for years even though he hated doing it. While in Philadelphia, he was approached by Daryl Spencer, a good hitting infielder for the Giants. He said, "Hey Al, if all those things you say are true you could quit biting your fingernails."

Daryl's words hit Al like a sledgehammer. The new Christian was taken aback by his teammate's remark. He went where he was somewhat alone and prayed, "Lord, help me to stop biting my nails. I don't want to hurt my testimony with Daryl. Please help me, Lord, to stop." From that moment, Al never bit his nails again.

Back home in Redwood City, Shirley was doing a lot of thinking about what had taken place in Al's life. She began to seriously doubt that any relationship she previously had with God was the real thing. She knew she had to do something about it. She went to a Methodist minister for spiritual help and came away empty. Not giving up, she went to see a Presbyterian minister but came away without any satisfactory answers. Having been raised a Roman Catholic; she went to talk with a priest. Disappointed, she returned home.

Her heart was crying out for spiritual help. Finally, in all sincerity, she took the Bible and got down on the floor with it in front of her. There was no doubt in her mind about God's existence but she knew she did not have the right relationship with Him.

The small pretty wife and mother said to the Lord, "God, if You answer the questions for me that I have in my heart, I promise You that I will trust You and give my life to You. Please help me." With steady hands, Shirley opened the Bible and began to read. All of a sudden, there it was right before her eyes. God in a wonderful way led her to open the Bible at the page that contained her answer. There on the floor, Shirley humbly prayed. As best as she knew how, she opened her heart to Christ and He became her Savior. She, too, became a new creation in Christ like her dear husband. God took their house and made a home out of it.

31

MY FRIEND, FELIPE

Al's road trips took on a new meaning now that the Lord was in control of his life. When in his hotel room alone, he would spend precious time with the Lord.

"One time in Cincinnati," he said, "I was so moved by the Holy Spirit, I could hardly contain myself. I cried tears of joy realizing anew how Christ died for me at Calvary. I was hoping my roommate would not come into the room. I went into the bathroom and cried out to God thanking Him for His love for me. I felt an outpouring of the Spirit of God on my life. I will never forget that wonderful experience. I often wonder how I ever lived without knowing the Lord."

All of Al's teammates knew of his conversion to Christ. It was the custom of a beer distributor to give a case of beer to each of the players when they returned home from a road trip. The same was true of a cigarette distributor. Al informed both that he no longer could accept their gift. He was determined there was not going to be any compromise with things that he thought were displeasing to the Lord.

The year of 1958 was the year that Al and Shirley will always remember. It is the year of their spiritual birthdays. Then, too, Al had what would be considered a good baseball year. He finished the season with eleven wins and seven losses. His earned run average was 3.64 and he appeared in 54 games.

The winter months passed quickly for Al and Shirley. It was time for another spring training at Phoenix. As always, the pitchers and catchers are among the first group to arrive. Al wondered how he would be accepted by his teammates. Would he have the joy of leading any of them to Christ? What did God have in store for him in the year of 1959?

When Al went to spring training, he was encouraged with his pitching. He had just had his best Major League winning season in 1958 with eleven wins. In 1955, he won 19 in the regular season for Minneapolis and six games in the playoffs including the Little World Series with the Rochester Red Wings.

In 1953, when he was brought up to the majors in the middle of the season from Triple A Minneapolis, he was confident that his ball was moving. He did what he did best. He threw low knee high fastballs that confounded both the Philadelphia Phillies and the hard-hitting Brooklyn Dodgers.

He could not shake off the mindset he had developed about his pitching. "The bad thing about it," said Al, "was that I took that mindset with me to the mound. The next thing I knew, I was developing stomach problems as well. My stomach ached and I didn't know what to do about it. Shirley said it was tension and she was right.

I really was creating my own problems by worrying about my fastball. I had so much for which to be thankful. I had a wonderful wife and three beautiful children. I was doing what I loved and getting paid to do it. Best of all, both Shirley and I were

Christians. Even with all of these blessings and more, I carried the worry baggage into the season and it really took a bad toll on my pitching."

One of the very special blessings of the 1959 season was Al's friendship with Felipe Alou. Felipe had played with Phoenix in the Pacific Coast League. He was one of the many fine players from the Dominican Republic. The 1959 season was the beginning of his great baseball career of seventeen years in the Major Leagues as a player. Felipe was the older brother of Matty and Jesus who also played Major League ball.

The Giants broke camp and were playing pre-season exhibition games with the Cleveland Indians as they traveled east. As Al tells the story, "It was April 7, 1959 and we stopped over in Des Moines, Iowa, for one of our exhibition games with Cleveland. I stepped out of the elevator one day and saw Felipe Alou sitting on a sofa reading a Bible. I walked over to him and said, "Felipe, are you a Christian?" Felipe looked up at me and said in his broken English, "No, I am not a Christian but I am going to be one."

"To me," said Al, "that was like opening the door for me to enter. Felipe became a spiritual challenge to me. Our friendship blossomed into a good relationship between us. We were together every day after that. I gave him a number of booklets written by Dr. M. R. DeHaan, a great Bible teacher. Felipe would read them along with his Bible. A good friend of his in the Dominican Republic gave him the Bible and said, "Felipe, I feel so sorry for you – you must be born again."

Whenever I had the opportunity to ask him, I would say, "Felipe, are you saved yet?" He would look at me with his sincere facial expression and say, "No, I don't think so." My heart would ache for my good friend. I said to him, "Just keep reading, Felipe." I knew that Felipe was lost and I wanted to help him but didn't know how to lead him to Christ. I prayed a lot for him."

The days passed into weeks. Time was ticking on and Felipe was not saved. One day Felipe walked by Al's hotel room and saw the door open. The Giants were in Los Angeles to play the Dodgers. He walked into the room and said, "Al, what else do I have to do?" Al looked at his friend and said, "You don't smoke, do you?" Felipe answered, "No." Al continued, "Felipe, you don't drink either, do you?" Again, Felipe answered no. Al said later that the two questions he asked his friend were dumb because they had nothing to do with salvation.

"Alright," said Al, "Let's see what the Apostle Paul told the Philippian jailer." He took his Bible and opened it to Acts 16:31 and began to read to his friend, "Believe on the Lord Jesus Christ, and thou shalt be saved, and thy house." Felipe believed in Jesus but he was not saved.

Al said, "Felipe and I talked every day about the Lord. He was still reading his Bible as well as Dr DeHaan's booklets. He was very open to the Gospel and it seemed at times, he was right at the doorstep ready to make his decision to accept Christ. Like I said, I didn't know exactly how to lead him to the Lord."

Al liked to shag fly balls during batting practice. One day while out in the outfield chasing down fly balls, he saw Felipe running out to him. About 25 feet away from Al, Felipe stopped and turned to watch the hitter. Al walked over to his friend and punched him on the shoulder. He looked at Al with a broad smile. "Felipe," said Al, "have you been saved?" "Yes," said Felipe who had come to know Christ through Al's testimony and the reading of God's Word.

Later on the Giants went into Milwaukee to play the Braves. Al thought it would be nice to have Felipe meet a black pastor. He looked one up and asked if he would join him and Felipe for a meal. Al was the only Christian, as far as he knew, that Felipe knew in the States. He thought it would strengthen Felipe to meet another Christian.

During the meal, the pastor told Felipe that he needed to be baptized. For some reason, the pastor thought that Felipe would not go to heaven if he was not baptized. In his broken English, Felipe said, "I am not going to be baptized in this country. Many Christians are persecuted in my country. I want to be baptized there so all can see me."

Al said, "Felipe was like Babe Ruth is to us. He meant a great deal to his country. He had only been saved two weeks and already had that boldness and courage for the Lord." Felipe spoke many times around the San Francisco area. Once he went to

Venezuela and a newspaper headline read, "Felipe Alou Arrived With Bible Not Bat."

Once on a plane, Felipe sat by me and mentioned two fellows on the team who had wanted him to go to church with them on Sunday. Felipe said, "I no go to church with you-you never talk to me about going to church until Al talk to me." Felipe was bold.

32

NO RELIGION ON THE FIELD

"Stealing baseball signs on the field is part of the game," said Al. "I don't think that using the scoreboard or other such mechanical means is right to do. I knew our team was doing that and I didn't feel right about it. I went to the manager and told him that I could not play with a team that cheated. As a result the manager stopped it."

Al did not do well in the 1959 season. He was in a total of 42 games. He started three and had a win-loss record of two wins and three losses. Al said that it was the only bad season he had. He did have 45 strikeouts in 73 innings, however. His stomach pain remained with him after the end of the season. "It really hurt," said Al. "I knew I could not pitch with my stomach hurting the way it did. Shirley and I and the children went home to Alabama."

Al was disappointed in his poor year for the Giants. He was thankful, however, that his stomach pains had subsided. Once again the winter months seemed to pass quickly and before long it was off to Phoenix and spring training. " I really didn't know what to expect. When I got the word that I was traded to the Boston Red Sox, my stomach aches returned."

He said, "The day I was traded to the Red Sox was a heart hurting experience. The Red Sox had their spring training camp in Scottsdale, Arizona. One day, we went over to Phoenix to play my former team, the Giants. Billy Jurges was our manager. As Boston was taking batting practice, he came out to center field where I was shagging fly balls. He walked up to me and said, 'I don't know how we got you because you are a pretty good pitcher. But I hear that you bring your religion on the field with you. I don't care what you talk about but don't bring your religion on the field. We play baseball on the field.' He then walked away."

"I got the point," said Al. "I should have said something to him about all the many trashy conversations I have heard on the field that had nothing to do with baseball."

The new Red Sox pitcher stood watching his former Giants teammates. He looked at his Boston uniform and then looked at the Giants. He thought to himself, "That's where I belong."

After Al got saved, he had such a great desire to tell others about the Lord. He said, "When I saw all those fans in the stands I felt like jumping up on the dugout roof to tell them about Jesus and what He did for them."

Standing in Fenway Park and looking out at the Green Monster didn't do much for Al. He felt that he really did not belong to the Red Sox. The Red Sox didn't use him much that spring. On April 15 after 28 days with the club, they sent him to Minneapolis where he had had a wonderful season in 1955. He was in only six games for Boston where he won none and lost one.

Being sent back to the Minors was a very happy occasion for Al. One big thing the move to Minneapolis did for him was to take away his stomach pain. In fact, he said, he was never bothered again by it.

Going back to Minneapolis was like going back home for Al and Shirley. It was Shirley's home State and Al had one of his best years in professional baseball there. That good feeling returned to Al and he felt like his old self.

The fans could not have been any better then they were to Al upon his return. The pitcher from Alabama, who in 1955 led the league with 19 wins and complete games with 18, was back home. He also tied for the league lead in games started. They had their Allan Fulton Worthington back and were expecting great things from him. Al did not let them down either. Of the eleven games he started, he completed nine of them. He appeared in a total of 37 games winning eleven and losing nine. The hard throwing right-hander pitched in 150 innings, giving up 117 hits and having only 34 earned runs scored off him. He struck out 100 and had a fantastic earn run average of 2.04. Those statistics would please most pitchers.

The Boston Red Sox, who still owned Al's contract, even though he was with Triple A Minneapolis, were very pleased with the good season Al had. It put a bigger value on him. Al was not pleased at all when he was informed that he was sold outright to the Chicago White Sox.

"It was not one of my better days," said Al. He was alone because Shirley had already gone back home to Birmingham to put the children in school. What a difference it meant to Al to be able to commit the situation to the Lord. He did not know his future but he now knew the One who held his future. God's Word was truly his comfort. He could turn to a verse like Romans 8:28 and put his entire trust in it. It reads, "And we know that all things work together for good to them that love God, to them who are the called according to His purpose."

Al knew that God was in charge of his life. He was determined that he would not stand in the Lord's way when it came to His directions for his life.

Many times Al cried out to the Lord to use him to reach the unsaved around him including his teammates. He purchased gospel literature to give to people, praying that God would cause them to read it and that they would come to accept Christ as their Savior. It broke his heart time and time again to see so many of his friends ignore the Gospel that is so simple that small children understand it and are saved.

Al's prayer was, "I'll try to be faithful to You, Lord, in telling others that salvation is only in You." Since he entered professional baseball, Al met many who were religious but lost. Everywhere he went, he found players, managers, coaches, front office people and fans who had religion in their lives but not Christ.

33

TAKING A STAND

He packed up his things and went to Chicago. In telling the story, Al said, "It was my fourth day with the White Sox in September, 1960. One of the pitchers told me that we had a man in the scoreboard with binoculars who was stealing the signs of the opposing team's catcher. He would then send what the pitcher would be pitching to the batter by way of a light in the scoreboard. If it was going to be a breaking pitch like a curveball, the light would flash on and off. If it was going to be a fastball, the light stayed on.

"When I found out what was going on, it really upset me. I like to win but I don't want to win if I have to cheat to do it. A call came to the bullpen and I was sent into the game and won in relief. After the game, we flew to Kansas City for a makeup game. The next day in the lobby of the hotel, I got the opportunity to talk with our manager, Al Lopez. He was definitely a veteran baseball man with 19 years in the majors as a player. In 1977, he was inducted into the Hall of Fame in Cooperstown, New York.

I told my manager that it was cheating to have a man in the scoreboard to flash the pitches to our batters. He said, "Show me in the rule book where it is cheating."

I said, "Everything can't be put in a rule book. Later, I thought that if it wasn't cheating, then why keep it such a secret?"

Al was not against stealing signs on the field. He realized that was just part of the game. Being a pitcher, he knew how important it is to keep the batters guessing and off balance. He said, "Part of the game is to pick up signs from the catcher when men are on base. When second base is empty, the catcher usually puts down one sign but when there is a runner on second base, the pitcher and catcher usually change their signs. When that happens the runner is not sure what the pitcher is going to throw.

I felt terrible being on a team that had a system that was cheating. Like I said, I had no problem with our players stealing signs on the field. I did have a big problem with using binoculars from the scoreboard and flashing signs to the batters. As a pitcher, I knew it was hard enough to win a game without someone calling your pitches.

The next day when we flew back to Chicago, I stayed in my room most of the day wondering what I should do about the situation. I finally made up my mind. I knew I had to do the right thing as a Christian. The thought kept going through my mind that I was about to break my contract with the White Sox. Most baseball players work hard and long to make the big leagues and here I was ready to leave the team. I felt sick about the whole thing but I knew what I had to do.

The thought struck me that I might be going to the ballpark for the last time. I arrived at about 5:30 that evening and made my way to the manager's office. Needless to say, I was nervous as I spoke to the famous baseball man. "Al," I said, "I've come to tell you that I can't play with a team that cheats."

He looked at me and said, "Well, I happen to be the manager and you will do what I tell you to do." Al went on to say that his religion would not allow him to do something that was dishonest.

I said, "I respect you but I cannot stay with the team if we continue to cheat."

Here I was speaking in churches and to youth groups about such things as lying, stealing and cheating. I would emphasize that these things should not have any place in a Christian's life. If I continued with a team that was cheating, how could I give such a message? I had to take a stand. I even told Al that I would be willing to talk to the General Manger, Hank Greenberg, about the matter."

"Go ahead," he said. "Go on up to his office and talk with him." "I found myself in the office of one of the great sluggers of baseball. He was a man who hit 58 home runs coming within two of tying the famous Babe Ruth. Over thirteen years, Hank Greenberg hit 331 home runs. He was elected to the Hall of Fame in 1956."

Once inside the General Manger's office, I said, "Mr. Greenberg, I came to tell you that I have to leave the White Sox because of what I believe to be cheating in stealing signs from the scoreboard and flashing them to our batters.

I also told Mr. Greenberg all I knew about Moses, which wasn't much. I wanted somehow to leave a testimony with him.

He told me that I needed to do what the manager asked me to do. I knew I could not obey my superiors. They didn't understand that Jesus is the Captain of the team that I belonged to and pleasing Him was priority number one.

Mr. Greenberg sent me to talk with the owner, Bill Veeck, a very intelligent man. It was the first time that I had talked with Mr. Veeck. I hardly said anything because he did most of the talking. When I saw there was not going to be a change, I knew I was finished with the White Sox.

I went to a telephone and called Shirley. If anyone would understand, it would be my wife. Walking away from baseball was a traumatic experience. That evening I flew back to Alabama. After I got home, my pastor came over to our house to hear what happened. As I related the story to him, he said, "You didn't have to quit the team. You didn't do any cheating."

"I was really surprised to hear such a comment from a preacher. It's pathetic how some Christians look at sin. I may not have been in the sign stealing system but I was with those who were doing it. I wanted nothing to do with the appearance of evil."

Actually, Al was not the one who publicly broke the news about the sign stealing. A Birmingham paper told how Ted Williams had discussed the matter with a sports writer. He described how a light would flash from the scoreboard so the hitter would know what the next pitch would be. When told about Williams' comments, Al was pleased that someone else, especially a famous player like Ted Williams, exposed the truth about the sign stealing system first. Al said, if God can use a famous player like Ted Williams to bring out the truth, the least I could do was to back it up.

34

A NO HITTER

Al was in a dilemma. He said, "I had a wife and three children, and no job. I enrolled at Samford University in Birmingham. The school was about twelve miles from our house. As I traveled to and from school the words of an old hymn, "God Will Take Care of You" filled my thoughts and came forth from my lips." The words are as follows:

"Be not dismayed whate'er betide, God will take care of you;
Beneath His wings of love abide, God will take care of you;
Through days of toil when heart doth fail,
God will take care of you;
When dangers fierce your path assail,

God will take care of you;
All you may need He will provide, God will take care of you;
Nothing you ask will be denied, God will take care of you;
No matter what may be the test, God will take care of you;
Lean, weary one, upon His breast, God will take care of you;
God will take care of you, Through ev'ry day,
O'er all the way;
He will take care of you, God will take care of you."

Even though Al was going to Samford University, he knew he had to find work. He took a part time job in what was called the Baptist Building in Birmingham. His working hours were from 4 p.m. to 10 p.m. It was a place where doctors, nurses, and other nearby workers come to relax, play games, watch TV, or even eat. When January came, Al had to make a decision to continue going to school or try to get back into baseball. When he did not seem to have any leading, he signed up for another semester of schooling.

When sports writers called Al to ask him what happened, he did not want to sound like he was a little boy who took his glove and went home because he wasn't happy with the White Sox. He did read in the paper that the White Sox said he quit because he wanted more money. In Al's words he said, "Man can't tell the truth. It wasn't the question of money at all. It was the question of honesty."

Al and Shirley prayed that the Lord would show them what to do. Finally the answer came. The Chicago White Sox, who still owned Al's contract, contacted him in May through the San Diego Padres and asked him to report to the San Diego Padres immediately. San Diego was in the Pacific Coast League.

"We packed our bags," said Al, "and in our Cadillac that we purchased in New York in 1957 for $800, we headed for California. It was a grand car with plenty of sleeping space for our children. On long trips like that, we usually stopped for the night around 3 p.m. Shirley wanted the children to have some time to play before dark.

The club paid for my way but they did not pay for the family so we traveled by car. I not only wanted my family to be with me but I needed them. We finally arrived in San Diego." Al had not played in the Pacific Coast League before. It was Triple A ball just like the American Association where he played with Minneapolis. The other Triple A league was the International League.

The San Diego team was made up of players from some three Major League organizations. The General Manager of the San Diego Club was Eddie Leishman whom Al described as a kind man. In fact, when the Major Leagues expanded, the General Manager said, "How could anyone pass up Worthington?"

Al mentioned that they had a dog that made it difficult for them to find a place to live. "No one seemed to want us because of the dog," said Al. "I was determined not to get rid of the dog. We finally found a place and it was lovely. Once again, the Lord provided for us and the kids could have their dog."

Two days after their arrival in San Diego and finally finding a place to live, Al had to leave with the team for Honolulu. He was so exhausted from driving from Alabama to California, looking for a place to live and getting his family settled in, he could hardly think straight. It was a flight of five and one half hours to Honolulu. Al said that he slept just about the entire trip. He was sitting beside one of his teammates and didn't even know him. "It was embarrassing to sit beside him for over five hours and not say hardly a word to him. I slept most of the time."

The 1961 part time season with the Padres was a good season for Al. It kind of made up for the short stints he had with the Red Sox and White Sox. He was hired primarily as a relief pitcher but actually ended up the season doing more than relief pitching. Hank Greensburg, with whom Al talked when he left the White Sox, spoke of Al as a pitcher "with a major league arm."

Manager Bill Norman decided to take full advantage of Al's "major league arm" by giving him a regular starting turn on the Padres' last road trip. Three appearances in a row, Al beat Spokane 12 – 0 with four hits, then stopped Hawaii 3 – 0 on four hits and then at home, pitched a no-hitter against Hawaii. The big right-hander was written into the San Diego Padres' record book with his no-hitter. It was the first no-hitter pitched by a San Diego pitcher in the 25-year history of the club. It was also the first no-hitter pitched by home or visiting teams in the four-year history of Westgate Park.

Manager Bill Norman said, "I sure was happy for Al, especially since I told the White Sox a few days ago, they should call up Worthington because he's one of the best pitchers in the league."

There was a rumor going around from one of Al's former employers that Al was not interested in talking about baseball. It said that all he talked about was religion. When Bill Norman got a hold of the rumor, he did what he could to put it to rest. He flatly refused to accept the rumor about Al. Norman said, "No, Al has talked to me about baseball."

Al's response was, "Why should I not talk about baseball? That is my livelihood. And why shouldn't I talk about Christ? He is my life."

Al can look at his time with the Padres and be pleased. He pitched in 28 games winning 9 and losing 10. He had 74 strikeouts in 109 innings pitched. With the season over, it was back home to Alabama.

35

GOOD SEASON AT INDY

With the Lord directing his steps, Al literally saw God's Word come true in his life. The following verses are just a few that Al experienced: "Trust in the Lord with all thine heart and lean not unto thine own understanding. In all thy ways acknowledge Him, and He shall direct thy path." (Proverbs 3:5,6), "The steps of a good man are ordered by the Lord: and he delighteth in his way" (Psalms 37:23), "For we walk by faith and not by sight." (II Corinthians 5:7), "I have chosen the way of truth." (Psalms 119:30a), and a verse The Holy Spirit led him to shortly after his conversion, "There hath no temptation taken you but such as is common to man: but God is faithful, who will not suffer you to be tempted above that ye are able; but will with the temptation also make a way to escape, that ye may be able to bear it" (I

Corinthians 10:13). The greatest response that Al and Shirley ever made to any verse was their response to John 3:16 which reads, "For God so loved the world, that He gave His only Begotten Son, that whosoever believeth in Him should not perish, but have everlasting life."

Since that miraculous event took place in Al's life in 1958, he had been preaching and testifying of the greatness and goodness of God. His greatest desire was to see people come to know Christ as their Savior.

Al was confident in the Lord and he knew that as long as he walked daily with Him that God would not allow him to make a mistake with his life. In fact even before he informed the White Sox that he could not play for them any more because of the cheating situation, God had impressed upon Al he would return to the Big Leagues some day.

Unknown to Al, his next year in baseball would be looked upon by him as one of his better years. Still owned by the Chicago White Sox, he was optioned to the Indianapolis Indians, a team in the American Association of which Al was very familiar having played with the Minneapolis Millers.

"It was really a good year at Indianapolis," Al commented. "I know the Lord was in my going there. We won the pennant easily. We got out in front of the rest of the league and just kept going. There were only six teams in the league. Every time I pitched, it seemed the hitters knew what I was throwing."

While playing for Indianapolis, Al, Shirley and the children attended Lifegate Baptist Church pastored by Dr. Ford Porter. Al said, "What a blessing to be there." That contact started a good relationship with the Porter family that has gone on for many years.

Al said he remembers well the time right after he got saved in San Francisco when a widow lady whose husband was a pastor, gave him the gospel tract, God's Simple Plan of Salvation. "That was the first gospel tract that I had ever seen," said Al. "I read it through four times as the wonderful truth became increasingly clear to me. It is so simple for one to be saved. There is nothing one can do to earn everlasting life. Jesus paid it all for us when He died on the Cross at Calvary, being made sin for us as we read in II

176

Corinthians 5:21, "For He hath made Him to be sin for us, who knew no sin: that we might be made the righteousness of God in Him."

He said that the tract impressed him so much that he contacted Lifegate, Inc. and ordered 1,000 of them. Al did not know it at the time but it was the beginning of many orders to purchase that small piece of paper through which countless thousands have come to accept Christ as their Savior.

Dr. Ford Porter, with the help of others, founded Indiana Baptist College that later became Heritage Baptist University. It was Dr. Ford Porter who wrote the very famous well-known gospel tract, "God's Simple Plan of Salvation." His son, Robert Porter, and grandson, Mark Porter, continued on with the tract ministry, known as Lifegate, Inc. For many years, Al has purchased Dr. Ford Porter's tracts for his personal tract ministry.

Al said, "My family and I enjoyed the year of 1962." During the 1962 season, Al pitched in 30 games. He won 15 and lost 4. In innings pitched, he led the league with 217 and had 149 strikeouts. His earned run average was a low 2.94.

36

NEXT STOP-
CROSLEY FIELD

On November 26, 1962, Al became the property of the Cincinnati Reds and started the 1963 season with the club. The city of Cincinnati has hosted professional baseball longer than any other city in the United States. As far back as 1876, Cincinnati fans have enjoyed watching organized baseball.

There was much written about Al in newspapers far and near. A lot of it had to do with his leaving the Chicago White Sox. Al knew that the only way to prove that he was major league caliber was to prove it with his pitching.

In the spring training exhibition baseball season of '63, Al was selected to pitch against the World Champion New York Yankees.

The Cincinnati Club decided to purchase Al for $25,000 from the White Sox who optioned him out to Indianapolis. His 15 – 4 record at Indianapolis placed a good value on him. The 34 year-old right-hander silenced the Yankee bats with one hit in seven innings.

In looking forward to the '63 season, he said, "I think I'm a much better pitcher today than I was with the Giants. Why? Because, I've got more knowledge and more pitches."

During the first month and a half of the season, Al owned an excellent 2.25 earned run average after 13 appearances in relief pitching. One sports writer said that Al gave a first of what was to come in the Grapefruit League. He yielded only one earned run. Speaking to a reporter, Al said, "I'm a slow starter and I always have been. You might say I get better as the season progresses."

The writers covering the Reds wrote openly of Al's faith in Christ. One writer described Al's preaching as being simple and forthright. He said that the right-hander was becoming almost as well known in pulpits in the area as he is on the mound at Crosley Field. Upon coming to the Reds, Al spoke at the City Gospel Mission, numerous area churches, youth groups, the Christian Businessmen Association breakfast meeting, and many others. As one article heading read, "When not pitching...Worthington preaches."

As far as being busy for the Reds, Al appeared in 50 games and ended the season with a 4 – 4 record. He pitched in 81 innings, struck out 55, and had an earned run average of 3.00. It is important to mention that he was extremely busy in his commitment to speak for the Lord in every opportunity that was open to him. Winning souls to Christ was the priority in Al's life.

The baseball season begins with spring training for the players. Once again Al found himself in the Red's camp in Tampa, Florida. Again, he was the subject of many interviews. How would he do in 1964? It didn't take long for things to start happening. Al appeared in six games for the Reds, winning one of them. When the cut off date of May 15th arrived, Al was sent by Cincinnati to San Diego. He stayed with the Padres long enough to appear in ten games, winning four and losing one. He pitched 34 innings and struck out 30.

37

CINCINNATI - SAN DIEGO - MINNEAPOLIS

In June, Al got word that Cincinnati sold his contract to the Minnesota Twins. Al and Shirley liked the Minnesota fans very much. Shirley was going back home again.

Their baseball related travels had taken them many thousands of miles by plane and car. They lived both on the east coast and west coast and many places in between. Since being saved, God had given them spiritual fruit all over the country.

It is expensive to travel and Al was wondering how he would get his family from San Diego to Minneapolis. The Twins, of course, would pay Al's plane fare but not for Shirley and the children. At this point, Eddie Leishman, the General Manager of the Padres got together with Calvin Griffith, the owner of the Twins and worked it out for the entire Worthington family to fly to Minneapolis.

Looking back over his years in professional baseball, Al has many memories some of which were unpleasant while others enjoyable and nice to think about. He still gets a laugh out of Hall of Famer, Roger Hornsby's remark. It is reported that the famous ball player said that Al should be playing ball with the Salvation Army's league of girls. Later on it was said that he called the New York Mets and encouraged them to buy Al's contract.

Al can laugh about it now but it wasn't funny then. The Giants were playing the Cardinals in St. Louis. The date was August 8, 1953. Al had a 2 – 0 lead going into the fifth inning. When the inning was over, the Giants were behind 3 – 2. A walk did the damage; two infield hits, a double, and an error that the paper called a mental lapse by Al. Runners were on second and third. Solly Hemus, the Cardinal shortstop was on second representing the tying run.

Red Schoendienst, the Cardinal second baseman, hit a grounder toward first and was called safe by umpire Larry Goetz. The runner on third scored and Hemus went to third. In disgust, Al stood with his head down holding the ball. The third base coach sent Hemus home while the crowd yelled. Hemus scored the tying run.

The papers said that Solly Hemus was able to score because Al was so intense in his argument with Larry Goetz. Actually, Al said that he never argued with an umpire. He just stood there with his head down. He does not deny that it was a mental lapse on his part but it was not because of an argument. "That is baseball," said Al.

Thinking of the past, one of the many events that stands out was a game between Al's team, the New York Giants, and the Chicago Cubs on May 3, 1957. The Giants set a record for the most players used by a team in a single game. The Polo Grounders used 25 players. The Cubs did not do so bad themselves using 23 players. The total of 48 players produced a winner for the Giants when they beat Chicago 6 – 5.

Al and Shirley were ready to settle down and stay at the same place for a while. "I feel comfortable here in Minnesota," said Shirley. "This is my home State and I like the colder weather. I can remember when I was a girl in Fulda how at times the snow would be up to the second story window. When it was like that we would climb out the upstairs window and slide down on the hard crusted snow. The men would shovel through to the front door." Hearing stories like that would make Al shiver.

One of the many stories that brings a smile to Al's face is concerning Jim Kaat, who became his close friend. At one point in their ministries, Al and Jim traveled for two weeks together giving their testimonies in churches, youth groups, etc.

Calvin Griffith paid out $25,000 to get Al and liked immediately what he saw. In his first two appearances with the Twins, Al, in five innings, did not allow a run. In those five innings, he gave up one hit and picked up a win and a save. At 35 years old, Al was pitching well. He struck out five and only allowed one walk.

A newspaper article said that Al, along with newcomer, Jim Snyder, from the Twins' Atlanta (International) farm club, broke in like gangbusters when they reported to the Twins. The article went on to say that Al arrived just two hours before the final of a four-game series with the White Sox. He came into the game in the sixth inning with one out and the score tied, 3 – 3. The newcomer from San Diego retired the side and gave up only one hit over the last three innings. The Twins finally won the game 9 – 3 giving Al his first win for the Minnesota Twins. Manager Sam Mele, did a lot of smiling with the addition of new faces on his '64 roster. Among them, of course, was big Al.

Al had come a long way from the young man who tried his best to get into professional baseball with Detroit, Atlanta, and Nashville.

With the Twins, one major thing in Al's favor was that the owner, Calvin Griffith, liked Al's pitching ability and believed him to be a good asset to the team.

As the season progressed, Al's value to the team became more and more apparent. Working out of the bullpen, the appearance of Al on the mound created an increasing confidence among the

Minneapolis fans. As was mentioned previously, Al was no newcomer to them. He came to the assistance of all of the Twins' hurlers, but he and Jim Kaat, especially, had a close working relationship as well as a good friendship.

Sam Mele used Al, the fast becoming veteran, as an example showing the importance of experience on the field. He said you can't beat experience on the mound in late-inning trouble.

When the Twins took a 3 – 1 game from Baltimore, Sam said that he wasn't a bit worried when Al walked Brooks Robinson and then went to 3 and 1 on John Orsingo in the eighth inning. "I knew the next pitch was going to be low for a strike," said Sam. He went on to say that with a youngster pitching, he would almost bet the pitch would be high and a ball in that situation. He said, "You can't beat know-how in relief." The veteran manager could read experienced Al like a book.

Al finished the season with the Twins in good fashion. He had a 5 – 6 win/loss record, appearing in 41 games. He struck out 59 in 72 innings. His earned run average was a phenomenal 1.38. Even though Al lost one more than he won, he said this was his best year in six and a half season of Major League baseball.

The Minnesota Twins was a team that Al enjoyed and felt good about. Friendships made with players like Jim Kaat, Jerry Kindall, Dick Stigman and Jim Perry, were good for the players and their families. Some of the friendships would last the remainder of their lives.

With the season over, Al went back home to Birmingham where Shirley had already gone to put the children in school. This time, however, he was excited about being the property of the Minnesota Twins and the good possibility they had to go all the way in 1965.

The opportunities were many for Al to share his testimony of what Christ had done for him. He loved to speak in churches and especially to youth groups. Al would say that when a young person got saved, it was not only a soul saved but also a life that could have years of service for the Lord.

First year in pro-ball

1963 Cincinnati Reds

First picture taken as a Giant

No-hitter
with San Diego

Record performance against
the Dodgers
July 11, 1953
Record still stands

Voted pitcher of the year
1964

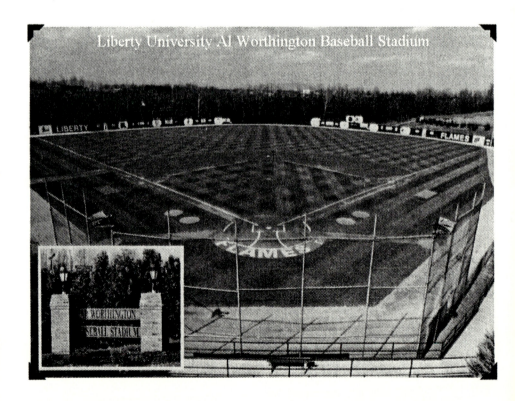

Liberty University Al Worthington Baseball Stadium

Al in action

University of Alabama 1950

Happy to be with the Twins

38

A PROMISING YEAR

As the Twins gathered early in the year for spring training at Tinker Field in Orlando, Florida, the air seemed to bristle with excitement. To the man, 1965 was going to be their year in American League baseball. For Al, personally, it was great to be playing for Minnesota. He was excited over the honor given to him during the winter. At the third Annual Mid-Winter dinner of the Twin Cities Chapter of the Baseball Writers Association of America, Al was voted the Twins Pitcher-of-the-Year. The amazing thing about the honor paid to Al is that he did not have the full season with the Twins but joined them in June of 1964.

"I was not with Shirley in Birmingham when our son, Marshal, was born," said Al. "I was in spring training and it was not expected of me to leave the team. Back then, a player did not

189

go home and spend a week or more with his wife until the baby was born. So on March 18, 1965, baby Marshal increased our family to six.

Once Marshal arrived, I could concentrate more on my pitching. In fact, to go along with my sliding fastball and mixture of breaking pitches, I worked on a knuckler, which I had used now and then for several years. I have disliked some spring training camps in the past but this one was different. It was hard work but a lot of fun getting ready for the upcoming '65 season."

Even though there were discouraging things that happened, the spirit of the team was upbeat. Numerous sports writers relegated the Twins to a second division finish. Few gave them a chance for fifth and even fewer for fourth. The team seemed to be hit with misfortune and uncertainty. To begin with, they were rained out of their opening workout on February 23. The Club President, Calvin Griffith, was hospitalized with a blood clot in his leg. Two main pitchers, Jim Kaat and Camilo Pascual, were holdouts. Second baseman, Bernie Allen, was slow in recovering from a knee operation and catcher, Earl Battey, developed a sore shoulder. There were positive responses to every negative thing that showed up. The team unitedly continued to work together as a solid unit.

There were other negative things that happened but the positive side seemed to be gaining ground. On April 30, the Twins took over first place for a day. On May 30, they took first place again and stayed there for 28 days. On June 6, their first place lead was three and one half games. The up and down Twins found themselves in third place on June 28 but only a half game behind the White Sox and Cleveland.

It was encouraging to Al on a personal basis to have Shirley, along with her parents, attend nearly every game. Her parents had moved to St. Paul from Fulda where Al pitched semi-professional baseball for the Fulda Giants, a team operated by Shirley's Uncle Dick. For Al and Shirley, it was like a family gathering at the Twins home games.

In spring training, it looked like the core of the relief pitching staff would be Dave Boswell and Al.

In an early season game, the Twins were playing the Cleveland Indians. Dave Boswell was pitching in relief. In the seventh inning, Sam Mele noticed that Boswell was consistently getting his pitches high. With runners on first and second and one out, Mele summoned Al from the bullpen. Hard-hitting Rocky Colavito was due up. Rocky hit one of Al's low fastballs on the ground that resulted in a double play.

"You see what it means," Mele said, "when you can go to the bullpen for guys who can protect a lead." Boswell confirmed the manager's move to take him out of the game. He said that he would have preferred to stay in the game, "But the skipper is right about me dropping my arm now and then. It was the right move to get Al in there."

Al was noted as one who threw as hard in batting practice as he did in a game. He said that when he was pitching batting practice at Alabama University one time, he was laying the pitches over the plate so the batters could hit the ball. He said, "A guy hit a line drive that knocked me off the mound. The ball hit me right on the side of the head," The tall right-hander went on to say, "Never again. The only defense I've got is to throw the ball hard. Make them work to hit it good." Al said his teammates laughed thinking it was funny. He went to the hospital that evening to be examined.

Some of the most famous sluggers of baseball have refused to take their practice cuts against Al. He grinned as he said; "I'm not going to lay that ball in there for anyone. They've got to hit my good stuff."

One famous slugger said this about Al's batting practice pitching, "I'm not going up there and hit against that stuff. I don't really like to hit against Worthington. I prefer a pitcher who throws it straight." Johnny Sain, the Twins pitching coach, said, "a relief pitcher that comes into finish tight games all the time can't even experiment. There is no margin of error." The talk was that Al had too much stuff in warm-ups.

As the 1965 season crossed the halfway point, George Brophy, assistant farm director of the Twins organization, and chief Major League Scout, Del Wilber, were discussing the Twins. The two men had recommended to Club President Calvin Griffith, that he obtain bullpen pitchers Johnny Klippstein from Philadelphia and Al Worthington from San Diego. In fact, it was Wilber who highly recommended Klippstein and Brophy, who recommended Al. It so developed that as the Twins headed down the final stretch, the pennant chances for Minnesota seemed to rest on the right arms of Johnny and Al who had been throwing baseballs for pay for a total of 35 years.

Al had turned 36 years old on February 5 of that year and was enjoying the best salary paid to him up to that time in professional ball. He said at the Twin City's Winter Baseball Dinner earlier that year, "The contract I received from Griffith included a raise bigger than the whole salary I received in 1961 when I went to San Diego of the Pacific Coast League." Al was greatly rewarded for the short but good 1964 season.

Al's pitching contribution to the Twins' cause was something to be expected. As one baseball writer put it after a successful relief appearance by Al, "Worthington's work, of course, has come to be expected." Al was called 'the King of the bullpen' in 1964 and that title continued to remain with him into the 1965 season.

Al can't recall the date but it was during the 1965 season when it took place. Little did he realize it at the time but it would be the beginning of a ten-year ministry for him. He said, "My preacher friend, Pastor Warren Littleford, asked me to hold a baseball clinic at the church. I remember saying, a what? A baseball clinic was new to me at the time. The Yankees were coming to town to play us so I asked Bobby Richardson if he would join Jerry Kindall and me to do the clinic.

After one of our games, the three of us met at the Southtown Baptist Church In Bloomington, Minnesota. Jerry and Bobby spoke first. There must have been more that 500 people in the parking lot. We each had a mike and each of us told something about playing baseball. After that, we each gave a testimony of how we trusted Christ to save us. I was the last speaker and when I got through with my testimony, I gave an invitation for the unsaved to accept Christ as Savior. I then invited those who made decisions to come inside the church. Over 100 professed to accept Christ that day."

An interesting sideline to Al's story is that he and Shirley had a live-in girl who helped Shirley with the children. The girl had a brother, eleven years old, who attended the baseball clinic. When

192

his mother came to pick him up, she said to him, "Lee, did you learn a lot about baseball today?" He answered, "Mom, I learned more about Jesus Christ today than all the time I have been going to Sunday school."

39

PENNANT BOUND

By August 27, the Twins stretched their league lead to 8 ½ games. The baseball scribes, both friends and foes, applauded Al for the major part that he played in the league leader's successes on the diamonds around the American League.

One newspaper late in August had for its Sports Page headline, "Worthington in MVP Race." The publication went on to list the accomplishments of Al for that season. It was mentioned that up to that point in the season, Manager Sam Mele had called on Al 51 times to stop the opposition.

The paper went on to say, "Worthington must be recognized as a strong candidate for the American League's Most Valuable Player Award. It said that the stouthearted veteran had won ten games and had been credited with twelve saves. When told about the possibility of the award, Al said, "I never even thought about being a candidate. I don't think I'll even be among the first ten."

Unusual exciting games seem to stand out in Al's memory. One of the games late in the 1965 season was with the New York Yankees. The powerful Bronx Bombers were in a 3 – 3 tie with the Twins going into the tenth inning. The Yankees had the bases full when Al was called upon to put out the fire. He got the third out, ending the inning by striking out dangerous Elston Howard, the Yankees' catcher. Jerry Kindall, Al's roommate on the road, gave the Twins the win and Al his tenth victory with a broken bat single. When Al was asked if it felt good to beat the Yankees, he said, "Yeah, every win is good."

The possibility to win the pennant became increasingly better as the season began to wind down. When Jim Kaat beat the Yankees 9 – 2 on August 26, it gave the Twins a 13 – 5 season edge over the defending champs. One by one the teams in the league were being mathematically eliminated from the pennant race. Finally, needing a win to clinch the pennant, left-hander Jim Kaat went to the mound on September 26 and beat the Washington Senators 2 – 1 on eight hits. It was Jim's seventeenth win of the season. Catcher, Earl Battey, squeezed the last strike and rushed to the mound to pummel Kaat, who soon disappeared in a mob of teammates. The Minnesota Twins had won their first pennant in their short history.

When Al was asked to comment about the season, he said, "It was a great year, wasn't it? Yes, I'd have to say I had my best year and so did a lot of other guys on the club." And a good season Al had. He appeared in 62 games winning ten and losing seven. He pitched in 80 innings and had 59 strikeouts. His earned run average was an excellent 2.14. He had fourteen saves.

Twins manager, Sam Mele, paid a high tribute to his bench men. Instead of calling them utility men, which was a common term in baseball, the proud manager called them 'most valuable men' and valuable players they were throughout the season.

How did Al feel after the close of the regular season? He said, "My fastball still has good speed and moves. I've got a much-improved curve ball. I used to be able to throw a curve to a left-handed batter, but not to a right-handed batter. My curve has improved with age and experience.

I work in and out on the batters now, trying to hit the corners. I'm more of a spot pitcher than I was. Right now, I'm planning on pitching for the Twins again next season. My arm and body are sound."

Al was so thankful that the Twins purchased his contract part way through the 1964 season. His shuttle days were over as far as he was concerned. He felt at home with Minnesota and that is where he wanted to stay. His Major League shuttle stops included New York/San Francisco Giants, Boston Red Sox, Cincinnati Reds, Chicago White Sox, and the Minnesota Twins.

40

WORLD SERIES
AND SICK SHIRLEY

The National League Champion Los Angeles Dodgers showed up with their pitching and speed. When the first game ended, the score was Twins 8 and Dodgers 2. Jim Grant won the first World Series game that he had ever pitched.

The Twins with a score of 5 to 1 also won the second game. Jim Kaat, who won 18 games during the regular season, defeated the Dodgers and their 26 game winner, Sandy Koufax. It was now on to California for the next three games if needed.

Al and Shirley flew on separate planes to Los Angeles. Al flew with the team on a charter flight. "I thought I might have the opportunity to witness on the way out," said Al, "but it seemed like everyone was celebrating too much to talk.

The Dodgers surprised us by taking the third game of the series by the score of 4 – 0. In game four, the Dodgers scored early and never lost their lead. They won 7 – 2 and thus evened the series two games a piece. Game five was a blow out for the Dodgers as they beat the Twins 7 – 0.

This put the Dodgers one up on us," said Al. "All they needed was one more win and it would be over. Our trip back to Minnesota for game six was a sober one. What a difference from the trip going out. I'm sure all of us thought we would return home as the World Champions. We had the wind taken out of our sails, so to speak.

Going out, it was next to impossible to witness to any one. Coming back, however, it was easy to talk to them. The celebration spirit was snuffed out with the three straight wins by the Dodgers in Los Angeles."

Al was concerned about Shirley. She was not on the other chartered plane returning to Minneapolis. He said, "It was great to have had Shirley with me. She was a big encouragement even with the games not going well for us. On the third day, however, she felt very sick. Several of the players' wives suggested things she could take."

"I really felt sick," Shirley said. "All that I wanted was to get back to Alabama as soon as possible. Al had major responsibilities with the team and I realized that. I didn't want to do anything that would interrupt his pitching in those crucial games. I told him to just help me get to the airport. He put me on a bus to the airport. The exhaust fumes almost did me in. I was so sick I could hardly stand it. The bus finally arrived at the airport. The people at the ticket counter told me that I was too sick to get on the plane. They said I should go to the hospital. I pleaded my case as much as I could and finally got their approval to get a boarding pass. While I was sitting in the waiting area, an announcement was made for Mrs. Al Worthington to report to the gate counter for a telephone call. A couple sitting in the area recognized our name and immediately offered their help to me.

I told Al that I had my boarding pass and was waiting to get on the plane. I laugh now when I think of how I pleaded and begged to get on the plane. I said, Please let me on and give me a sack to throw up in and I'll be all right. I made it on the plane and settled back. The flight seemed extra long as I tried not to think how sick I was. What a relief it was to finally arrive in Birmingham.

Two of Al's sisters met me and took me to the hospital. I remember telling the doctor how bad I felt. All of a sudden the thought came to me to ask the doctor to check and see if I was pregnant. He did and we had the answer. I watched the rest of the World Series from my hospital bed."

The team arrived back home having their work cut out for them. They took the field that Wednesday, October 13, 1965, determined to beat the Dodgers and stay in the series. Jim Grant stood on the mound before a record-setting crowd of 49,578. The yelling, whistling, screaming, crowd was deafening. Al was stationed in the bullpen ready to come into the game if he was needed.

'Mudcat,' as he was affectionately called, did not need any help. He pitched a six hitter and helped his own cause with a home run. The 5 to 1 win tied the series at three games each.

The seventh game of the series was a squeaker. A record crowd of 50, 596 turned out hoping to see their Twins capture the greatest event in baseball, the World Series. It was not to be, however, as the Los Angeles Dodgers won 2 to 0. It took one of the best pitchers in baseball to put down the fighting Twins.

When Al returned home after the series, he had the wonderful feeling of being blessed with a full player's share of World Series pay of over $6.000. He had come a long way from his first paycheck with the Nashville Vols at Sulpher Dell. The Lord had priority in the lives of Al and Shirley and He was blessing them in their faithfulness to Him.

41

MAMA'S HOME-GOING - DANIEL'S ARRIVAL

One thing about Al that was well known to the press was that he was a family man. He did not like to be away from Shirley and the children. He did make a winter trip, however, to cold Minnesota to sign his 1966 contract with the Twins. When ice skating was mentioned by one of the reporters, the 37 year-old Al said, "I have already gone ice skating in the past and I thought I did pretty well. I skated once when I spent a whole winter here."

The year, 1966, was not only filled with baseball but also with blessings and testings. Coming off a ten win, seven-loss season was good for Al. In Orlando during spring training, Shirley and the children took things in stride. The very special baseball wife

203

said, "You might think it's kind of a nomad's life we lead, but I've enjoyed every minute of it. I say, I don't want to move anywhere for a month. But, you know, it's funny, when we get into February, I think of going to spring training again. And, if I'm not ready to pack, my daughter, Linda, tells me, Come on, Mother, we've got to start packing."

Spring training was coming to an end. Before departing North, they were scheduled to play an exhibition game with the St. Louis Cardinals. Just before the game began, Al received a telephone call. The caller told him that his mother had passed away. Being the kind of man he is, Al kept the news to himself. He put in his three innings of work. He knew that his mother would have wanted him to do that. His thoughts went back to Birmingham and the wonderful mother he had.

When the game was over, Al went to Manager Sam Mele and told him that his mother had died. Al was so thankful that he did not have to sorrow like those who have no hope.

Al's sister, Betty, and her husband, Jim Payne, had arrived to pay a visit with Al and Shirley, showing up after the game. The two families left together and went to the home of Al and Betty's parents. Of those who were gathered for lunch that day, Al was asked to pray before they ate. He said while he was praying, the Holy Spirit moved within Him in a wonderful way. Al prayed, "Lord, this is the worst day of my life but You are more real to me now than ever before except when I was first saved."

I felt so blessed in knowing I was saved and that Shirley knew and loved the Lord as well. I was thankful for the love I had for my family. The Lord gave me such wonderful parents. My mama was very special. Her love and devotion to her family was something that none of us would forget."

The Twins broke camp and headed North to Minnesota. Shirley and Al loved baseball but there were two priorities that were more important than baseball. They were God and family. On May 13, 1966, The Lord blessed Al and Shirley with another son. They named their newborn Daniel, who was born in Minnesota, the birthplace of his mother.

Al smiles when he points out that son, Allan, was born in January 1954, and the Giants won the pennant. Son, Marshal, was born in 1965, and the Twins won the pennant. He said, "In 1966, my third son, Daniel, was born and I began to tell everyone that we should win the pennant. The only thing is--it doesn't work that way."

42

ACCIDENTS DO HAPPEN

The Twins' management began burning up the telephone wires when the news reached them of Al's injury to the tip of his index finger and the middle finger of his right hand. He caught his hand in his garage door and immediately recognized the potential gravity of the injury as far as the team was concerned.

Team physician, Dr. Bill Proffitt, said that Al could be out of action for up to ten days. Al was thankful that there were no bones broken. The injury to Al, on June 28, started a chain reaction on the team. Starter, Dave Boswell, was assigned to the bullpen. Jim Grant was asked to pitch after two days rest. Manager Sam Mele said, "Worthington is not just another pitcher. It'll take a lot to replace him."

One writer pointed out that the accident happened on June 28-two years to the day when Al was purchased from San Diego of the Pacific Coast League, when the Twins were in another emergency. From being a Minor League pitcher, Al joined the Twins bullpen and was a big help to the team the remaining last half of the 1964 season. He went on to say that Al did a pennant-winning job in the bullpen during the 1965 season.

With Dave Boswell winning five straight and tied for the league lead in strikeouts at 137, the Twins were gaining momentum by the end of July. Again, Al was right in the heart of the action. It was taken for granted that every time he went to the mound, he would do well. One baseball scribe, in describing Al's relief pitching said that Al protected starting pitcher Boswell's ninth victory with his customary eighth and ninth innings of no-hit pitching.

At 37 years old, most Major League ball players have already retired from the game. President Calvin Griffith expressed his hope that Al would give him at least one more year. That would take Al through the 1967 season.

Al said, "I've got eleven credits left to get my college degree in Physical Education. I can't get all of them this winter at home in Birmingham."

In speaking about his bullpen relief ace, Manager Mele commented, "Al gets better with age. I'd hate to lose him permanently."

Taking in the whole picture, Al wanted the best thing for his family. He loved to play baseball and especially with the Minnesota Twins. His years with the Millers and then the Twins gave him a special relationship with the fans.

As for his most recent season, he looked back on what he would call mountain top experiences. Of course, anything done for the Lord took priority with Al. In baseball, however, there were many high spots throughout the season. How could he forget August 17 when he had six straight strikeouts against the California Angels?

Then there was the game in Boston on August 19 when Jim Kaat and Al teamed up to pitch a four-hitter. It was Kaat's 18th win and Al's ninth save. After the game, Jim told reporters, "That

Worthington has backed me up all year when I needed him. Of course, he's done the same for the whole staff, but I know he's helped me in at least three or four." Jim eventually won 25 games.

The 1966 season was another good productive season for Al. He was in 65 games and had a 6 – 3 won-loss record and eleven saves. Al's strike out total was 93 in 91 innings pitched. His earned run average of 2.47 was slightly more than the previous years.

43

TINKER FIELD TO CLOSE PENNANT FINISH

Tinker Field in Orlando was becoming a spring home base to Al. "I'm with Minnesota," he thought, "and I feel like I'm wanted." The 1967 spring training was underway. As usual, the pitchers and catchers arrived early so by the time the other players arrived, the pitchers were ready for intra-squad play.

In fact, on March 9, Al was asked if he wanted to pitch. He said that he would since it was his day to pitch batting practice anyway. The veteran pitcher had been in camp for only a week so really was not ready. Being the competitor that he is, Al went into the intra-squad game and retired nine of eleven batters. He said he threw different pitches including his knuckleball.

Al was never hesitant in giving praise where praise was due. For example, the Twins were playing the Chicago White Sox the latter part of May. It was a rather wild game that the Twins took 8 – 7. Al went to the mound in the ninth inning and got the first two men. Who then should come to the plate but the dangerous Smokey Burgess. He hit a 1 and 1 pitch and looped it into right field for a single. Al then retired the side when the next batter flyed out to right.

Speaking about Burgess, Al said that he was up there swinging all the time and that's what makes him tough. "He doesn't stand there taking anything," said Al. "He'll almost always get a piece of the ball. He's got a great eye, good timing, and you put those together and he's pretty hard to fool."

In mid season on June 9, Sam Mele was let go as manager and was replaced by Calvin Coolidge Ermer who was an experienced manager in the minors for seventeen years. The Sporting News named him Minor League Manager of the year for 1958. Ermer was trusted with the field leadership of the Twins who, just two years before had won the American League pennant.

Al knew very well that he was involved in a vocation that could bring unforeseen changes at any time. How thankful he was that his relationship as a child of God could not change. He had perfect peace not only in the saving power of Christ but also the keeping power of the Holy Spirit. Al's salvation was eternally secure. How he longed for his unsaved teammates to come to accept Christ as their Savior.

He thought of the tremendous burden the Apostle Paul had for his lost people and how he wanted that same kind of burden for the lost. The Apostle said, "That I have great heaviness and continual sorrow in my heart. For I could wish that myself were accursed from Christ for my brethren, my kinsmen according to the flesh." (Romans 9:2,3).

The Twins responded well to Ermer's leadership. They went from sixth place and a 25 – 25 won-loss record to be edged out by the Red Sox on the last day of the season.

Regarding Sam's dismissal, Al said, "I liked Sam. He possessed a lot of baseball knowledge. When a team is not producing, the manager is the one who becomes the target from the fans and the club's brass.

Well, we finished second and this meant some funds to be divided among us because of our second place finish. When it came to voting how the World Series shares would be divided among us, a number of us were disappointed in our teammates because they would not include our former manager for a share.

One baseball writer who no doubt represented the thinking of many other writers said, that we lost the respect of people in baseball by the cold heartless manner in which we dealt with Sam. There were twelve of us, however, who thought Sam should receive a full share."

Al, along with Dean Chance and Earl Battey talked and talked but their talking could not sway the opposition. The twelve teammates, who were willing to dip into their own pockets, if necessary, were Earl Battey, Dave Boswell, Rod Carew, Dean Chance, Jim (Mudcat) Grant, Harmon Killebrew, Billy Martin, Tony Oliva, Cesar Tovar, Sandy Valdespino, Zollo Versalles, and Al Worthington.

Al said later that the funds came from the World Series share to the Twins and not from their own pockets.

Looking back on his season, Al thought he did all right for a 38-year-old pitcher. He was in 59 games and won eight and lost nine. He pitched in 92 innings, struck out 80 and had an earned run average of 2.84.

44

TIME TO RETIRE?

It was always good to have several months at the end of the year to do some speaking in churches, youth groups, and other meetings. Between the end of one baseball season and the beginning of the next spring training was always a busy time. This time was no exception. Al finished his studies at Samford University in Birmingham for his Bachelor's Degree. Showing his customary smile, Al said, "I crammed four years of college into twenty years." At 38 years of age February 5, 1968, Al was referred to as the "Pappy" of the team.

When he reported for spring training at Tinker Field in Orlando, Florida, Al was in the best shape of his career, which started back with Nashville in 1951. A baseball writer describing

Al and his contribution to the Twins since his purchase in 1964 said Al was credited with 227 relief appearances and had a win-loss record of 29-25 up to the start of the 1968 season. He spoke of Al being active in The Fellowship of Christian Athletes. He mentioned in his information piece that Al was a Baptist and that his favorite pastime was giving out Gospel tracts. When asked who was his favorite person in history, there was no hesitation by Al. Even as a small boy, he wanted to be like Jesus even though he did not know Him as his Savior at that time.

When it came to asking Al about baseball and who were the toughest hitters he faced, he named Jackie Robinson as number one and Stan Musial second up to that time. He also named Wes Covington, Ron Hansen and Roger Maris. It would be interesting to ask the batters in the Major Leagues who faced Al as to the toughest pitcher they faced. Al would not say this but some of them would no doubt mention him. Surely in individual games, he would be mentioned by some of the hitters from the Phillies and the Brooklyn Dodgers, when he shut them out and in doing so, gave up only two hits to Philadelphia and four hits to Brooklyn back in 1953.

At 39 years old, Al was well respected around the league for his pitching skills. A good example of his pitching abilities was demonstrated early in the season in a game with the Chicago White Sox. The date was April 26. His roommate on the road, Jim Perry, was the starting pitcher. Perry ran into trouble in the sixth inning and was relieved by Al. The Twins scored three runs in the third inning. With a 3 – 2 edge, Al struck out the White Sox' three, four, and five batters with the bases loaded in the seventh inning to save the one run lead.

In fact, he struck out Pete Ward, Tommy David, and Russ Snyder on eleven pitches. With the win, Jim Perry's record stood at 2 – 1 for the young season. Al was 0 – 0 but had three saves.

The local newspapers did not hold back at all from printing stories about Al's faith in Christ. One baseball scribe wrote that when the Twins arrived in Detroit after just beating the Red Sox 7 – 6, Al was happy both ways. If the Twins win, he was happy inside and outside. If they lost, he may not have been happy on the outside but he was happy on the inside. In other words, Christ was his true joy and gave him inward peace.

Al said, "Baseball isn't my life. Sure, it's my livelihood and it's important to me. I love to play baseball and have considered staying in the game in some capacity when I'm through pitching. It might sound strange for me to say baseball isn't my life."

He went on to say, "Jesus Christ is my life." Al could not separate Christ from baseball nor could he separate Christ from his home life. He said also, "That's why I can't think it's all over if we lose a ball game."

Regarding his future, Al said that he did not hold his future, but rather, Christ held his future. In playing baseball, he simply wanted to do his very best; using the talents God had given to him for the Lord's glory.

By May 12, the Twins were three games from the league leading Detroit Tigers. Al and Ron Perranoski stood out as the bread and butter pitchers. Perranoski had 3 – 0 for his record and Al had eight saves. By May 27, Al had gained his tenth save. Of the 110 saves recorded by Minnesota since Al joined the club in the 1964 season, he had recorded 62 of them.

With the season coming to a close, there was increasing talk about it being Al's last playing season. It was commonly known that Al might teach or try coaching. He said, talking to reporters, "I haven't tried to keep it a secret that I'm leaving baseball. I made it known pretty well since June, when I couldn't throw too well and my control wasn't too good. Why am I quitting? Well, for one thing, I want to stay home with my family more. Then I've noticed the hitters weren't so easy to get out anymore. I've thrown some pitches up there this year that I could hit. I knew then it was time for me to get out."

The newspapers, as they had been with Al, gave him excellent coverage including both his outstanding pitching and his testimony for the Lord. Al has a wonderful memory that was tested at the end of the season. He was asked if he remembered his first game as a Twins player. Al was quick to respond by saying, "My first game as a Twin was June 28, 1964. It was a Sunday afternoon and I relieved Dick Stigman in the sixth or seventh inning against Chicago. The next inning our big bombers hit a few home runs

217

and I got the victory, 9 – 3. My first save was two days later at Baltimore. I relieved my roomie, Gerry Arrigo. We won that one, 3 – 1."

Al also remembers his first loss in a Twins' uniform. He said they were playing the New York Yankees on July 4 at Yankee Stadium. Mickey Mantle hit a three run home run late in the game. The Twins lost 7 – 5. Al said that he remembers that game so well because first base was open and he could have walked Mantle.

Al told reporters gathered about him, "I'm retiring with many wonderful memories of the treatment I received."

A local paper wrote, "Worthington, a devoted church and family man, picks from baseball association his most gratifying experience." Al said, "In 1958, while with the Giants, I met Billy Graham and gave my life to Christ. I was saved."

For the 1968 season, Al appeared in 54 games. He won four and lost five. He pitched in 76 innings and had 57 strikeouts. He had another respectable 2.72 earned run average.

45
BACK IN UNIFORM

Returning home after the baseball season was over was not anything new to Al. The big difference this time, however, was that the 39 year-old seasoned veteran was coming back home for good. As far as Al knew, there would be no more spring training and no more traveling from city to city to play baseball. The call 'play ball' and the roar of the fans would be gone.

The once anxious young man who tried so hard to get into professional baseball now could look back over eighteen years of pro ball. During that time he wore five different major league uniforms and was in the majors for all or part of thirteen baseball seasons.

Just because he had retired from baseball didn't mean that Al retired from what he loved to do best – witness for Christ. Many wanted to hear him tell of his conversion, his witnessing to fellow

Major League players, how he was told that the ball field was no place for religion, the time he left the Chicago White Sox because he did not want to be associated with cheating.

Al had numerous opportunities to preach in churches, speak to youth groups, and men's fellowships. Turning Al loose in the pulpit with his Bible or out on a crowded street corner with Gospel tracts caused the same kind of excitement in his heart. He loved to tell others about Jesus Christ his Savior and what a change He made in his life.

With spring training underway, Al called and talked to Jim Perry and Jim Kaat, two close friends, who encouraged him to come back. Al said, "I talked to Billy Martin during spring training and told him I might be available. He responded by telling me to keep in shape in case I was needed."

A sports writer calling for Billy Martin called Al in the middle of May and asked him to think about returning to the Twins. When he called back a couple of days later, Al said that he would return. "When you feel like you're wanted," said Al, "it is easy."

At 40 years old, Al was in good shape, physically and mentally. "I had three jobs that I was busy with at home so it wasn't like I was just loafing around or being a 'couch potato,'" Al commented. "I like to be actively involved in things."

Despite no spring training, Al was near ready to go when he joined the Twins. He said, "missing spring training hurt at first, because everybody was ahead of me. I have a girl who graduated from high school already, but I can still pitch and I'm extremely glad to be back here."

Al also said that the prospects of a possible playoff and a World Series check could have had something to do with his return. So in less than a year of retirement, Al was back in uniform.

His performance did not reveal anything about him missing spring training and joining the team after the season started. On July 16, 1969, the Twins took a double header from the White Sox stretching their league lead over Oakland by five games. Al had already registered four wins since his return. Twins catcher, John Roseboro, who was a ten-year major league regular, said it had been a long time since he'd seen anybody strike out three men with the bases loaded. Al responded that he would have to go back at least ten years when he was with the Giants. At that time, he struck out three Philadelphia batters with the bases loaded.

In one of the local papers, there was quite a long article on which pitcher in the American League would you like to have on the mound in the following situation. The bases are full with one out. You are one run ahead in the last of the ninth. There is no place to put a batter. You need a strikeout. Now the question is, what would you do? The article ends, "Just ring the bullpen and ask for Al Worthington." That is the respect that Al had at age 40.

Shirley, too, was busy doing what was dear to her heart. She had the joy of attending the Minneapolis Christian Women's Club. Mrs. Jim Kaat, wife of Twins' pitcher, Jim Kaat, was the club president. Mrs. Jim Perry, wife of Twins' pitcher, Jim Perry, also attended the special event. They got a nice write up in the local papers.

The Baltimore Orioles easily took the American League Eastern division and then beat the Western Division champions The Minnesota Twins, in three games. The New York Mets then took the Orioles four games to one in the World Series.

For Al, he was in 46 games, winning four and losing one. He pitched in 61 innings for the Twins and struck out 51 opposing batters. His earned run average was higher than usual at 4.57. This would turn out to be Al's last year as a major League pitcher.

With the season over, Al and Shirley went back to their home in Alabama. As far as a job was concerned, Al decided to sell life insurance. In a conversation with a company representative, Al was being told about the various kinds of policies. After hearing the man out, Al asked him a question. He said, "Do you have any eternal life insurance policies?" The man looked at Al with a confused look on his face. He had no idea what Al was talking about. It certainly was a perfect way to begin a witness about the Lord.

221

46

BASEBALL CLINICS

The baseball clinics ministry kept tugging at Al's heart. He loved to get before a crowd of young people and talk about baseball and then end the clinic telling about Christ and the salvation He purchased for us through the shedding of His blood on the cross.

The seed was planted well with the first baseball clinic with Bobby Richardson and Jerry Kindall back in 1965. The Baseball Clinic Ministry had such a grip on Al's heart, it was just the normal thing to plan and look forward to the next one.

Well, the next one was for the summer of 1966, Al said, "The first one (1965) started me and it became an automatic thing for me to do. As a player, I never wore my Twins uniform when I held a clinic. After my career ended, I wore the uniform to draw the crowd. In 1970 and 71, I left Alabama and took the family back to Minnesota to hold clinics. Pastor Warren Littleford made out an itinerary for me for the two summers. I held two clinics a day. There was one in the morning and one in the afternoon. They were usually both in the same area.

The clinics usually were conducted about the same way. Now and then adults would show up as well. As always, I would talk about baseball then for about twenty minutes, I would give them the Gospel. The response was tremendous. Seeing 45 out of 50 make decisions was normal. Al said, "I trust I will see many of those boys and girls in heaven."

Al loved baseball and enjoyed playing it but there was no joy that baseball gives to compare to leading a boy or girl to Christ.

One time as Al was leaving a church where he had spoken to a group of young people, a lady stopped him in his car to talk to him. She asked, "Did my son talk to you?" Not knowing her son, Al said, "No." The lady went on to say that her son got saved in one of the clinic meetings.

His second retirement year from baseball, 1971, was another blessed year in baseball clinics in reaching primarily young people. Again, Al was doing what he loved best. It wasn't until his tenth year of holding baseball clinics that Al began to meet those who were saved in earlier years.

He was in a church one summer and an elderly man came and shook Al's hand. He said to Al, "Did my grandson talk to you?" Al answered that he had not talked with him. Later, a big strapping sixteen-year old fellow came to Al. He told him he was saved in one of the clinics. It put Al on cloud nine. That same year, Al was in a church in St. Paul, Minnesota. "A man came up to me," said Al, "and told me that his daughter made a decision in one of my meetings. He brought his daughter over to introduce her. Standing before me was a beautiful sixteen-year old girl who had made a decision to accept Christ in one of my meetings seven years before."

As he carried on his clinics in Minnesota, Al could not help but think of some of the happy experiences he had in baseball. One of those was his friendship with Watson Spoelstra, a sportswriter for the Detroit Free Press. Watson, who was called

'Wally' by many, was once an alcoholic. It is told that his daughter was near death and Watson told God that if He would let his daughter live, he would live for Him. The Lord healed Watson's daughter and being true to his word he accepted Christ as his Savior. The former alcoholic became a new creation in Christ Jesus as the Apostle Paul wrote to the Christians at Corinth. He wrote, "Therefore if any man be in Christ, he is a new Creature, old things are passed away, behold all things are become new." II Corinthians 5:17.

One of the ministries that Watson established was to conduct Bible services for Major League ballplayers. He would appoint a couple of players on each team to get a meeting room at a hotel and invite the players to come. A pitcher who came to the Twins from the Los Angeles Dodgers told Al that Watson asked him one time to help arrange a service. He arranged for a meeting place and encouraged his teammates to come. Little did he realize that he would get saved after listening to the message from God's Word. Watson Spoelstra had a tremendous ministry and was a wonderful blessing to many.

Al tells about holding a clinic during the summer of 1971 under a shade tree. He said, "I started the clinic in the shade of a big tree, two boys climbed the tree to watch and listen from there. All of a sudden, a car pulled up about thirty yards away. A man and a boy got out and walked toward me. He stopped to listen to what I was saying. After I finished with my message, he brought the boy to me. He said that ten years before, he brought his other two boys to hear me speak in the area. I asked if his two sons were saved. He said they were and that is why he was bringing his third son." In the summer of 1971, Al was beginning to see wonderful fruit from the past years.

Al's life, since his conversion in 1958, was filled with both positive and negative experiences. It was not unusual for him to pull a story out of his past at any time. The story of Don Mingo is one of those that stands out in Al's memory.

47

DON MINGO

Don, himself, tells the story. He said, "It was the 1965 baseball season-Dan Patch Days in Savage, Minnesota. Dan Patch was the greatest two-wheel buggy racehorse of all time.

I'd been drinking most of the day. I started drinking when I was in the Navy. In fact, I was up to a quart a day of alcohol and constantly getting worse. My life was out of control and I did not even realize it!

I started home from Savage so drunk that I could not steer my car and ran it into a ditch. It was dark but I managed to get out of the car and make it up the bank to the highway that was 135 West. I started hitchhiking and a car stopped to pick me up. The driver was Al Worthington, the outstanding relief pitcher for the Minnesota Twins. In fact, the Twins won the American League pennant that year. Al's pitching was a big help to the pennant winners.

As we drove toward Minneapolis, Al told me about Jesus. He mentioned how he was going to heaven because Jesus saved him. I didn't understand much of what he said. I replied in my drunkenness, 'Yeah, yeah, I know all about it.' He was polite and as he dropped me off, I believe he prayed, "God, please help him."

It was fourteen years before I heard the old story again. My mother had died at age 52. My life was on a runaway track to hell. I was in and out of jail, drunk most of the time, and just running, running, and running.

It was at that time that my oldest son, who was graduating from Bible college, told me the same old story. He told me how he was saved and going to heaven. He told me how I could be saved. With a pocket full of gospel tracts, I went home to seek after that which I knew I did not have, and that was the peace I saw in my son's eyes.

The Holy Spirit was working in my heart and on June 21, 1979, I got saved. I then remembered that night in 1965 when Al Worthington had planted the seed of God's Word that grew until I became a child of the King of Kings.

After I got saved, I began looking for Al and I think it was Thanksgiving week that I learned that he was Athletic Director at Liberty University in Virginia. I wrote him a letter telling him my story, we wrote back and forth and in the exchange of correspondence, he sent me his baseball card with his testimony on it. We are friends and brothers in Christ.

God called me to preach in 1982 and I served Him at the Milwaukee Rescue Mission from June 1982 until 1988. Over a four-year period, we brought in 42,000 young people. I have had the privilege to preach in South America, Ukraine, Moscow, Cuba, Canada, Mexico, and throughout the eastern half of the United States. We have seen over 25,000 souls trust Christ as Savior and to think that the gospel seed was first planted when as a drunk, I crawled out of the ditch and was picked up by one of God's servants, Al Worthington, pitcher for the Minnesota Twins. I praise God for saving me and giving me the blessed opportunity to serve Him."

48

PITCHING COACH FOR TWINS

"That fall, Mr. Calvin Griffith, President of the Twins, called me," Al said, "and asked me to come back to be his pitching coach. The love for the game and the fact that this was something I believed I could do caused me to accept Mr. Griffith's offer. We were already in Minnesota because of the baseball clinics so there was no big move for my family. I thought it would be pretty exciting to see what I could do with the pitching staff and especially with the younger ones.

His call and the job offer came out of the blue. I certainly was not expecting such an offer. To be honest about the offer of the job and a salary of $17,000, that was a poor wage, but I knew the Lord was in it.

According to a local newspaper, I inherited a terrible pitching staff. I had two good pitchers who were friends of mine on the team. I had roomed with both of them so knew them quite well. Bill Rigney was the manager but was let go after a couple of months. Frank Quilici took over as manager.

I began holding meetings with my pitching staff. In fact, I had some of the other players talk to them as a group - Harmon Killebrew and Frank Quilici were two of them. I recall what Frank said one day. He told them, "When you throw a pitch and the umpire calls it a ball, don't look like he missed it. You walk around on the mound like the umpire was responsible."

Al said the 1972 Twins were really not a great team. He did say the pitching staff that year set a club record with a 2.72 Earned Run Average. I thought our pitching staff did a wonderful job in helping us finish third.

It is my belief that pitchers need to run a lot. I remember in spring training, we were to play Houston at 10:00 A.M. in Orlando. Jim Kaat, who was to pitch that game, stood on the dugout steps with me. It was about an hour before the start of the game. I said to Jim, "Jim, you need to run." He said, "I'm pitching." "Yes," I said, "I know but we just got out of our beds, your body is not ready for you to pitch."

Jim went out on the field and ran in the hot sun. He came back later and changed his wet clothes. That day, he gave Houston only one hit. Al said, "Pitchers need to run a lot to keep their legs in shape."

Back in the fall of 1972, Al called to speak to Dr. Jerry Falwell, the President of Lynchburg Baptist College in Lynchburg, Virginia. Dr. Falwell was away from campus at the time so Al left a message with a secretary. He told her to tell Dr. Falwell that he knew they needed a baseball coach and that he would like to be that coach. When Dr. Falwell returned, he called Al and invited him to come to Lynchburg to talk with him and to see the school.

Al said, "I knew three years before we left Birmingham, that I was going to leave Birmingham but I didn't know where I would go. I knew that Shirley and I committed our lives to the Lord and He would direct our paths."

Knowing they would eventually sell their home in Birmingham, in early 1972 Shirley asked the Lord that when it came time to sell that He would cause the first people who looked at the house to buy it. That is exactly what happened.

49

LEAVING PROFESSIONAL BASEBALL - MOVING TO LYNCHBURG

Al told Mr. Griffith that he would be leaving the Twins when the '73 season ended. Shirley went to Lynchburg, bought a house, and enrolled the children in school. Al arrived the end of September. That was not a surprise to Al's followers as Dr. Falwell let the news out on his TV program.

It was a big change for Al to go from pitching coach for the Minnesota Twins to head baseball coach for the Liberty Baptist College Flames. The school later was renamed Liberty University.

In his thirteen years as head coach of the Flames his teams compiled a record of 342 wins and 191 losses.

After thirteen years as head coach, Al stepped down to turn the reins over to former New York Yankee second baseman great, Bobby Richardson. Richardson took over the coaching job in 1987. To honor Al for his splendid work of building a strong baseball program at Liberty University, Dr. Jerry Falwell, LU's Chancellor, renamed the baseball field, Worthington Field. Al expressed his feelings by saying, "It was one of the great honors that has come my way."

Al looks back on his accomplishments at Liberty and is pleased that he took his team to three consecutive appearances in the NAIA World Series from 1981 to 1983. He coached Liberty University teams to twelve 20 plus win seasons. His team, the Flames, won 40 games in 1983 and achieved Division 1 status.

As Al thought of his 16 1/2 years at Liberty University, he enjoyed talking about the accomplishments of his teams and individual players. "Three of my boys played major league baseball," he said. "They were first baseman Sid Bream and pitchers Lee Guetterman and Randy Tomlin. It gives me a certain satisfaction to know that they achieved the very highest in professional baseball. It was a privilege and a joy to coach them.

As long as I am giving credit to where credit is due," continued Al, "I want to express my appreciation for all the boys I coached. They wanted to play ball and they were willing to commit themselves to learning the fundamentals of the game."

Al broke out with a grin when he spoke about his start at Lynchburg. He said, "When I went to Lynchburg in 1973 to look things over, I asked when I could see the baseball diamond. I was told there wasn't any baseball diamond. I wondered where we would practice and play. Well, we practiced at a field that the City of Lynchburg gave us permission to use. It was the worst baseball field that I ever walked on.

One of my players built a big broom that we fastened on the back of my old Valiant car; we then dragged the broom around the infield. It made the field look better but it still wasn't that good. We practiced there from 1974 to 1979. When Sid Bream came, I knew we could not practice there any more. Sid was a big strong left handed hitter who would hit the ball out of the field on to a road filled with traffic. Someone was bound to get hurt or even killed.

I felt so sorry for my players at that particular field. They had to change into their uniforms in some very filthy bathrooms. The fellows wanted to play so much that the filthy bathrooms and rough field didn't seem to bother them."

The games were played at the City Stadium but the problem there, was that the Flames were listed fourth in priority for field use. The professional baseball team in Lynchburg was first. Even the high school team had priority over the Flames."

Al said, "I caught myself one day thinking how nice it was in the major leagues. There was carpet on the clubhouse floor, shoes were shined, and there was always a clean uniform. Here I had the equipment packed in my car and so many things were different.

All of a sudden, the Lord impressed upon my heart. He reminded me that He had prepared me for this job even before I went to Lynchburg. After the Lord dealt with me, I looked at the situation in a different light. Even those peanut butter sandwiches that we ate for lunch before our away games had never tasted so good before.

I told my players that we were to be grateful for the practice field the Lord gave us to use. They were so hyper in wanting to play ball, it would take a lot more than what they faced to discourage them. They were just great guys and I enjoyed coaching them."

One thing that really was a great blessing to Al was that some fifteen of his players responded to the call of God on their lives and went into full time Christian service. There may have been more that Al didn't know about. "I loved my job coaching and teaching the fundamentals of baseball but my greatest reason for coaching and working with the young men was to encourage them to live dedicated lives for the Lord and be willing to follow His direction for their lives. If Christ is not in it, then it is not worth doing."

He told about a conversation with Johnny Klippstein one day when they both were on the roster of the Minnesota Twins. "We were leaving the bullpen together when Johnny mentioned something that I really appreciated. He said, 'Al, do you realize that there hasn't been any dirty jokes told in the bullpen for the two years that you have been here?'

I thought how my testimony for the Lord affected the lives of the other players to the extent that they were careful in what they said in my presence."

During his 16 1/2 years at Liberty University, Al thought many times how fortunate he was to work in a sport that he loved and be paid for doing it. He especially enjoyed working with Christian young men and women who represented such wonderful potential for the Lord.

He revealed his thoughts by saying, "It was an ideal place to serve the Lord. We had students from foreign countries that would, after graduation, go back home and be a witness for Christ among their own people. Talk about having a ministry in missions that reached around the world, I saw it at Liberty."

50

I PLAYED AND I WON

On December 15, 1989, Al and Shirley said goodbye to Liberty University. "I knew my work was finished there," said Al. "I had 16 ½ wonderful years there and I believe I left a good spiritual influence on many precious lives. I left on good terms with the chancellor, Dr. Jerry Falwell, and the president, Dr. A. Pierce Guillermin. Our children were in the south and we felt that we wanted to be closer to them. Like I said, we had those many blessed years at Liberty, but it was time to take the next step for what the Lord had for us."

As Al and Shirley went back to Alabama, they did so with countless memories that had accumulated over the years. One of those outstanding memories for Al was when the Minnesota Twins' fans twice voted him as the all-time Twins' Relief pitcher.

The first ceremony took place at the Carleton Celebrity Room in Minneapolis on July 31, 1986. The Twins Silver Anniversary Team in 2000 included such greats as Harmon Killebrew, first base; Rod Carew, second base; Zollo Versalles, shortstop; John Castino, third base; Bob Allison, left field; Cesar Tovar, center field; Tony Oliva, right field; Jim Kaat, left-handed pitcher; Camilo Pascual, right-handed pitcher; Al Worthington, relief pitcher; Earl Battey, catcher; and Billy Martin, manager.

Not a day went by but what memories of the past occupied the thoughts of Al and Shirley. The most important memory for each of them was when they accepted Christ as their Savior.

"That was definitely the turning point in our lives," said Al. "As I think of the countless numbers of people without Christ, I have to believe that for many of them, it is a matter of pride. Unbelievers just don't want to humble themselves before Almighty God.

The Psalmist wrote, 'The wicked, through the pride of his countenance, will not seek after God: God is not in all his thoughts.' Psalms 10:4. The Bible says that Jesus Christ, 'made Himself of no reputation, and took upon Him the form of a servant, and was made in the likeness of men: and being found in fashion as a man, He humbled Himself, and became obedient unto death, even the death of the cross.' Philippians 2:7-8.

Christ, who took part in creating all things, who owned the universe, willingly came to earth, born of a virgin, and as a man, God's son, died for the sins of the whole world. The Bible tells us, "And Jesus called a little child unto Him, and set him in the midst of them, and said, Verily I say unto you, except ye be converted, and become as little children, ye shall not enter into the kingdom of heaven. Whosoever therefore shall humble himself as this little child, the same is greatest in the kingdom of heaven." Matthew 18:1-3.

In the book of James we are told, "Humble yourselves in the sight of the Lord, and He shall lift you up." James 4:10.

People who count on their greatness or riches or even their good works, cannot satisfy a Holy God. The rich man's millions, the great admired athletes, the academic geniuses, the powerful world leaders cannot rely on their accomplishments to gain heaven.

238

In order to please Almighty God, all must humble themselves before Him in order to be saved.

Pride is a tool of Satan that hinders man from acknowledging himself as a sinner and accepting God's plan of salvation through His Son, Jesus Christ. During my 21 years in professional baseball, I can recall perhaps ten players who gave evidence of being born again. Not many people in the world's spotlight want to humble themselves before God.

God's Word says, "For by grace are ye saved through faith: and that not of yourselves, it is the Gift of God: not of works, lest any man should boast." Ephesians 2:8-9.

Friend, if you have never accepted Jesus Christ as your Savior, I ask you to do it now. Whatever your excuse for not accepting Christ, is it worth ending up in hell? My heart's desire is to see people come to know Christ, whom to know, is life eternal.

As I look back over my years in baseball, I not only played, but I am thankful that I won – in Christ."

REFLECTIONS

I

SARALIL'S TESTIMONY

There are so many wonderful experiences and memories that God has given to Shirley and me. I would love to put all of them in my book but that would be impossible. One of those wonderful experiences that stands out took place in 1967. It happened during the winter in Birmingham, Alabama.

I was invited to speak to a youth group at the Trinity Methodist Church. Before the meeting, the young people were eating hamburgers and one of them offered me one. As I was sitting at a table eating, the associate pastor walked up and I was introduced to him.

He asked me, "Would you be willing to speak at our church service?" Before he could change his mind, I said, "I would be glad to speak." The pastor of the church was not there.

Al preached and gave an invitation. I believe there were nine who came forward with one of them being a woman by the name of Saralil Oliver Thompson, who later married Tom Cleage. Al said, "Little did I realize the tremendous woman that Saralil Oliver Thompson represented. Her future husband, Tom Cleage, sent me some of the details regarding Saralil beginning that very same evening back in 1967."

He wrote, "That night in December of 1967, Saralil Oliver Thompson, divorced mother of three felt drawn to the service at Trinity Methodist Church.

Her elderly mother, 'Pete' Oliver, had lived with Saralil and her kids since the divorce, and she had recently become a Christian through the ministry of Southeastern Bible College.

Saralil's mother had been driving her crazy with talk of Jesus, but this night 'Pete' was surprised to see her daughter preparing to go the Sunday evening service. Saralil hadn't attended in the evening since her teenage days in MYF. She was unable to give her mother an answer as to why she was going, she only knew she had to go.

Saralil's husband had left her three years earlier with three small children (ages 5,3, and 1) and with minimal child support. She had been a stay-at-home mom but she was now working three jobs, with no car, living tranquilizer-to-tranquilizer. When she was hospitalized for 'nerves' in the fall of 1970, a chaplain asked if she had given her life to Christ. She gave no clear response because she didn't understand what he was talking about.

Her life was in shambles and she didn't know which way to turn. She felt rejected by life and totally inadequate to be both mother and father to her children and to provide for their needs. Two weeks before Christmas that year she tried to be excited for the kids when decorating the house, but she felt painfully lonely. When they finished the Christmas tree, she felt supernaturally led to dress for church.

God had a plan for her and several others that night. As Al Worthington spoke and then gave an altar call, Saralil was compelled to go forward. She didn't exactly understand what was happening but she knew she had to have what Al had. He had described how he had everything there was to have in life; a wonderful wife and children, a promising career in baseball, but no inward peace. That personal relationship with Christ was not there.

Al told how he found the answer in Jesus Christ. He was there that night by divine appointment to walk Saralil through the gates of salvation. She was born again.

Unknown to her that night, her good friend Joe Morgan came forward also. He had married her childhood playmate and they were in each other's weddings. God worked mightily in these two over the years with Joe finally speaking her eulogy thirty years later, testifying to the wonders our Lord had done in and through Saralil since that incredible beginning.

Saralil believed that God had been standing at the door to her heart knocking for a long time, but she kept the door closed to Him. She came to learn, as C.S. Lewis had, that every story of conversion is the story of a blessed defeat. She felt that she had to suffer many disappointments –her 'defeats'– hopelessly exhausting her own efforts, before she would open that door.

But Saralil was not through suffering. The first year as a believer in Jesus, with circumstances unchanged, she repeatedly felt defeated trying to live her new Christian life. She questioned her salvation, whether God really did come through that door. But God was working in ways she could not see. Late in 1971, He led her and her mother to Briarwood Presbyterian Church where they would remain and flourish. This is also the church where Joe Morgan became an Elder and influenced many lives for Jesus.

At Briarwood, Saralil received instruction in the Bible and was taught how to live a victorious Christian life. She learned to seek God in His Word, through prayer and quiet time alone with Him, offering Him her praises and petitions. She also came to understand that fellowship with believers was vital to her walk with the Lord as was sharing her faith with others. She immersed herself in these activities and began to grow in her faith.

Saralil received godly teaching and wise counsel through her pastor, Frank Barker. She also received intimate, hands-on discipleship training in a group of single mothers led by Julia Fulkerson. Julia later married Mike Quarles, and they are today in fulltime Christian service with the Freedom in Christ Ministry. Julia was there in Saralil's hospital room thirty years later, ministering faithfully to her friend as she lay waiting to finally see Jesus.

In their discipleship group these women studied, prayed, and shared, seeing God's mighty provision in their meager circumstances. They prayed and rejoiced as God provided a car for Saralil and a job that would allow her to be home during the summers with her children. Saralil shared the story of her 'blessed defeat' with other single mothers, encouraging many lives.

Saralil became a mighty prayer warrior, talking with God throughout the day and beseeching Him continually on behalf of her children, friends and acquaintances. She had a gift of discerning the needs of the hearts of those she met, and she was an active minister for Christ in the day-to-day lives of those around her. During the fourteen years she was a single mother, God taught her that he would be her husband and take responsibility for providing all her needs.

In 1981 she remarried, becoming the wife of Tom Cleage, honoring and loving her husband as God had so graciously prepared her to do. She was blessed to feel that, over the course of the next twenty years, she was able to transparently model for her children and others what a godly marriage was supposed to be.

Her servant's heart never ceased in its ministry to others and her mother's heart never tired in her devotion to her children – Scott, Barri and Bryan. Her mother, Pete, was blessed to be nursed by Saralil for many years. Pete now enjoys the blessing of her eternal company in glory because God, in His wonderful grace, used Al Worthington to bring His message of hope through her daughter's open door so many years ago.

Saralil went to be with Jesus in March of 2001, after a lengthy battle with cancer. Until we join her there, we won't know how many lives were changed as a result of that one divine appointment. What a day that will be!"

God used Al in marvelous ways in reaching people for Christ. His ministry crossed denominational lines to touch the lives of those with spiritual needs. He was God's instrument in leading Saralil to the Savior. As Tom said about his wife, "We won't know how many lives were changed as a result of that one divine appointment." Yes, what a day that will be!

In thinking about that meeting at the Trinity Methodist Church, Al said, "I met a young girl at the Mayor's Prayer Breakfast later on who had been at the church meeting. When the breakfast meeting ended, the father with his nine-year-old daughter walked up to me. He had tears in his eyes as he spoke, He said that his daughter got saved that night at Trinity Methodist Church and came home and told him what happened to her. As a result, he accepted the Lord as his Savior."

II

THAT MIRACULOUS EVENING

AUGUST 22, 1963

Christians are attracted to Christians and with Al being a Major League baseball pitcher; he had many opportunities to speak to individuals as well as to groups about the Lord. He said, "One night in Cincinnati, I was sitting in the bull pen down the third baseline. I was seated on the bench with two of my teammates to whom I was witnessing. I looked up and here came a man out of the stands toward our bullpen bench. The bench was located next to the fence. When the man got to the fence he asked for Al Worthington.

I raised my hand and said, "I am Al Worthington." That night, I met Dick Ellis for the first time. He had heard that I was a Christian and he wanted to meet me. After about fifteen minutes he left and went back up into the stands. I looked at my two friends who were sitting there listening and said, "What do you think?" I was shocked at the answer I got.

One of them said, "I knew he was a Christian because of how his face shone." The second one said, "I knew he was a Christian because of the love in his eyes."

Al didn't think too much about his conversation with the stranger, as that was very common with him, not only at Cincinnati where he played for the Reds but also around the league.

Sometime later, a couple appeared at the Worthington home unannounced.

245

It was the same man who spoke with Al over the bullpen fence earlier in the season. This time he had his wife with him. Dick and Shirley Ellis were invited into the house where they spoke with Al and Shirley. Dick thought it was interesting that the two wives had the same name.

In their conversation, Dick said he would like for Al to come and speak at the church where he and Shirley attended. He said, "We want you to come and affirm what Shirley has been telling her class." The church did not have a Sunday evening service so a date was set for the evening of August 22, 1963.

On their way home, after talking with Al and Shirley, the couple was thrilled that they were able to schedule the major league pitcher to speak in their church. Shirley looked over at Dick and said, "Dick, God is really in this service!"

There was no doubt in the minds of Dick and Shirley Ellis that the Lord was arranging everything for them. "As soon as we stepped in the door of our house," said Dick, "Shirley called one of her closest Christian friends and prayer partners, Betty. She, in turn, started calling her friends to commit our upcoming event to the Lord in prayer.

We immediately went into action to pull things together and get things arranged for our upcoming speaker. We made a trip to Springfield, Ohio, where we talked with a radio station manager of the local Christian radio station. Don Hall, the station manager said that we would need to get the word out about the guest speaker who was coming. We knew other churches in the general area would be interested in hearing a Major League baseball player give his testimony. Don agreed to help us by being the Master of Ceremonies and sing a solo for the evening event. We gave him our information and the announcements went on the air right away. We were so excited to think of what the Lord was doing.

I contacted the Village Airs, a well-known gospel-singing group from Clarksville, Ohio. They usually were booked well into the future but that particular Sunday night, they had open for them to come and sing. The Lord was working things out.

We asked the Lord for the best for this service. One thing we needed was a good pianist. We contacted Mrs. Robert Walker of the Sabina Methodist Church. She was more than pleased to come and play.

My wife, who loves to entertain, felt that we should make our guest speaker a fine meal before he spoke. With the help of a few men of the church, she set up a large dining room in our finished basement. While she was preparing the meal, I went to pick up Al at the Cincinnati ballpark. There was a doubleheader that Sunday so we arrived a little late for dinner. Our guests numbering about 40 did not seem to mind at all that we were a bit late in getting home.

Soon after dinner, we left to go to the church. By the time we arrived, everyone was there waiting for us. The Lord blessed the announcements that had gone out over the radio and the advertisements in the newspaper. The church was packed. It was the first time as far as I knew that there was a Sunday evening service in the church.

When we entered the church, my wife and her friend, Betty, went to the basement to pray. It seemed that this was the first for several things in the history of the church. It was the first evangelistic service that I could remember. We were new to an evangelistic service so we were not sure what would happen.

I sat by my good friend, Pres Grey, and pretended I was going to listen to Al talk about baseball. I knew better, however, for we were about to hear something far better than baseball talk. The Village Airs sang and then, Don Hall, ministered to us in song. The atmosphere of the meeting was perfect for God to do something special among us. When Al walked to the podium to speak, you could sense the presence of the Lord. Al's friends from the Christian Business Men's organization from the Cincinnati area had been praying for this special meeting for some time.

The message Al gave was definitely directed by the Lord, as it seemed to be perfect for the audience that was there. The response to the message was tremendous. Thirty-four people came forward to accept the Lord Jesus as their Savior. Since we were not used to such an evangelistic service, we had no trained counselors or even a room prepared for those who came forward. That didn't matter to Al. He dealt with them as they asked Christ to save them. One lady later remarked to us that she wanted to go forward to accept

Jesus, but she just couldn't get her legs to move. As soon as she got home, she knelt by her bed and accepted Jesus as her personal Savior.

The presence and power of the Holy Spirit was so strong in the building that the people who remained in their seats did not move or talk. They sat still observing what God was doing. It was a wonderful holy sight to see.

To those who came forward Al explained to them what had taken place in their hearts. As they prayed, they asked God to forgive them of their sins. Al told them that the blood of Jesus had washed their sins away and that His blood now covered them.

At the close of the invitation Shirley and Betty emerged from the church basement where they had been praying during the service. Shirley asked me, "What's going on with the people? They seem to be acting odd." I explained to her that they were simply reacting to the work of the Holy Spirit in their hearts. They had been touched and moved in the altar call. At the end of the service, Al passed out gospel tracts explaining again salvation in Christ and what to do next in their new walk with the Lord."

In speaking of that wonderful service, Al said that every member of the Don Moore family got saved that night. As a result Don and Georgia's five children became active in their churches as well as the grandchildren. A number of them went to Christian colleges and entered fulltime Christian service.

Georgia Moore wrote years later, "To think that all of this happened because of the love a young couple (Dick and Shirley Ellis) had after being born again and used the one person (Al Worthington) who God knew would woo us to Jesus."

III

A GREAT BIRTHDAY GIFT

"On February 5, 2004, which was my birthday, Shirley and I were driving to the airport to fly to Nicaragua, we stopped at McDonalds drive-in for something to eat. When the young black man opened the window to take my money, I recognized him. I said, "Son, I will not give you this tract because I have already given you two of them. Are you saved?" He broke out in a big beautiful smile. He fastened his eyes on me and said, "December 14th."

I said, "You mean you were saved on December 14?" He beamed with happiness. He replied, "Yes, I got saved."

The happy young man said, "When you came by here the first time, I didn't know what you were talking about." It was about five months earlier that I had gone through the drive-in. As the same young man opened the window to take my money, I gave him a tract and said, "This tract will not get you to heaven, but it will tell you what you must do to get to heaven."

The young man looked shocked, stunned and confused as he looked at the tract.

About two months later, I went through the drive-in again. He opened the window and I handed him a tract and told him the same thing I said the first time. I did not recognize him, but he said, "You already gave me a tract."

I said, "Take this one. Are you saved?" The young man looked at me and said, "No."

On February 5, 2004, and some five months after I gave him the first tract, God gave me a birthday gift. My young friend told me that he got saved. What a great birthday gift!"

IV

OVER ONE MILLION HEAR THE GOSPEL

Missions has played a big part in Al's life since his conversion in 1958. One of the many bright spots along the way was with the Gordon family. Jim and Diane, along with their son, David, and daughter-in-law, Brenda, became dear friends of Al and Shirley.

Al said, "For 16 years I went on short missions trips to Central and South America with Jim and Diane. They started a mission's organization called Sports and Cultural Exchange, International. Jim passed away a few years ago. His son, David, took over the ministry. What a tremendous opportunity to play sports and at the same time, give out the Gospel and see people come to Christ."

Al's face reflects the joy within his heart when he talks about how God opens doors for him to witness. He spoke of one such opening in Nicaragua in the year 2000. "David asked me if I would take part in a sports television show. I told him that I would be glad for the opportunity. At the television station we were informed that the program would be an hour long and that about one million people watched it daily. I sat for nearly 45 minutes without anyone saying a word to me. I tried to relax and be patient. Finally, I was called to the platform. The announcer brought out my baseball record and especially mentioned my experience with the White Sox when I quit the club. He said, "Al, we know you quit the White Sox for a moral reason. Would you tell us how to get to heaven?"

I almost fell over. For the next 15 minutes, I shared God's plan of salvation to about one million people. The White Sox incident happened in 1960 and this took place in 2000. The thought came to mind that God was not finished with me yet."

V

GONE OFF THE DEEP END?

In 1962, Al played for the Indianapolis Indians and, in fact, he speaks of it as a good year. He commented, "I won 15 and lost only four for Indianapolis that year. The ball club was having a special event. Two men from the Minnesota Twins organization showed up. They did not speak to me or I with them.

Later on, George Brophy, of the Twins and a friend of mine, called me and asked what college I was going to attend. I told him that I already was enrolled in Samford University, a Baptist school. George, like some others, thought I had flipped my lid and gone off the deep end. My friend, George, wanted to make sure that I was all right and thinking straight before the Minnesota Club purchased me.

The unsaved do not understand Christians. We are different. For one thing, a Christian who is living for the Lord, does not enjoy sin. Before we were saved, sin was our friend. We loved it. When Christ becomes our Savior, the bondage of sin is broken. No, I did not flip my lid or go off the deep end. I just love the Lord and want to please Him with my life."

VI

A NICE COMPLIMENT

Al told of a conversation with former major league player and manager, Bill Rigney. He said, "In 1968, we were in Anaheim playing the California Angels. The Angels' manager, Bill Rigney, heard that I was leaving professional baseball after the season. He asked me if I wanted a scouting job. He then said, "We need more men like you in the game. We have enough of the other kind." That was certainly a nice compliment from my former manager."

VII

"A GREAT PERSON TO HAVE ON THE CLUB"

In 1988, Chuck Burch, Sports Information Director for Liberty University, wrote to Mr. Calvin Griffith, owner of the Minnesota Twins. His letter said that he was trying to do a compilation of Coach Al Worthington's athletic accomplishments.

He wrote, "Did you ever rate the Twins pitchers? If you did, how would Coach Worthington have fit into your rating?"

Mr. Griffith penned a note on the letter from Chuck Burch. It read, "Dear Chuck, Under my ownership, 1955-84, Al Worthington would be number one. Also, he was a great person to have on the club. My best, Calvin Griffith"

VIII

A DIVINE APPOINTMENT

The following reflection is a paid advertisement that Al wrote.
It was published in The Birmingham News on September 13, 2003.

Al Worthington, a former Major League baseball player, was converted to Jesus Christ during the Billy Graham Crusade in San Francisco, CA in 1958. For the past fourteen years, he has been a short-term missionary to Central and South America. This is a conversation that he had with a young woman named Mary Jane who is the assistant to the President of a University.

"Mary Jane, I would like to ask you a question. Has anyone ever told you the plan of salvation or do you know for sure that you are going to heaven when you die?"

Mary Jane said that no one had ever told her the plan of salvation and she did not know if she was going to heaven.

"Are you interested in going to Heaven?" "Yes, of course." "Would you allow me to tell you God's Plan of Salvation?" "Yes," she said.

We both sat down and I said, "Mary Jane, when Adam and Eve sinned in the Garden of Eden, man became separated from God because of sin. Man became a murderer, a drunk, a liar, a thief, he hated and coveted, etc. How does man come back to God?"

In I Timothy 1:15, Paul says 'Jesus Christ came into the world to save sinners.' The Bible says in Romans 3:23, 'All have sinned, and come short of the glory of God.' The word 'all' means everyone in the world. From working at the University you receive a wage for your work. God says in Romans 6:23 'For the wages of sin is death. Because we are sinners, our wage is death. In Revelations 20:14 the Bible tells us what death means. 'And death and hell were cast into the lake of fire. This is the second

257

death.' Everyone knows the first death is when we lay our body down in six feet of dirt. You, I, and all the people of the world deserve hell for we have sinned against a Holy God. The good news, Mary Jane, is found in Romans 6:23 where the Bible says that the gift of God is eternal life through Jesus Christ our Lord. God offered the gift of eternal life to the whole world. Salvation is free. If you could work for a gift it would not be a gift.

In Ephesians 2:8-9, God has more good news. He says, 'For by grace are ye saved through faith; and that not of yourselves, it is the gift of God; not of works lest any man should boast.' The dictionary says grace means the freely given unmerited favor and love of God. It is God's grace we are born in America. We could have been born in a jungle somewhere. God is giving the whole world a chance to go to heaven. The Bible says that it is not of works lest any man should boast. There is not one person in heaven today who says, "I gave thousands of dollars to the church and I was faithful to the church and did many good deeds for many people. In fact, I think I will go to heaven because I am a good person." There is no one in heaven who can boast of anything they did. Heaven is a gift from God, not something that can be earned.

There are two things you must do to receive the free gift. Jesus Christ says in Mark 1:15 'Repent ye, and believe the gospel.' Repent means to be penitent for one's sins and seek to change one's life for the better. You must have a change of heart, a turning away from your sin. Let's say you are robbing one bank a week. You quit. Tell God you are repenting of your sin. You do not rob any more banks. You have a change of heart. Second, you must put your faith in what Jesus Christ did for you. He paid your sin debt.

I recently flew from Miami to Atlanta. I cannot fly an airplane so I went to an airline company who trains pilots to fly. I could have decided not to fly saying that the pilot could not fly well enough or the plane might break in two or the plane might fall. But instead, I bought a ticket to Atlanta. I trusted the pilot and the plane. I committed myself to them both. The plane got up to 30,000 feet and we landed safely in Atlanta." Jesus paid for your plane ticket to heaven (I John 1:7, Revelation 1:5). All you must do is receive Him. (John 1:12).

Mary Jane, in Revelation 3:20 Jesus Christ say, 'Behold, I stand at the door and knock; if any man hear my voice and open the door I will come in and sup with him.' The reason Jesus is not in your heart is that he has to be invited in. He does not force His way on anyone. You remember when we were little and we did something wrong. Sometimes our heart was pounding we were so scared. We knew it was wrong but we did it anyway. Remember? That was God saying don't do it, yet we would do it anyway.

Jesus Christ died in your place and He is knocking on your heart door. Will you turn from your sin and put your trust in Him?" "Yes," she said.

Mary Jane prayed and told God she was sorry for her sin and she was turning away from her sin. She asked Jesus to come into her heart and save her. After her prayer, I opened the Bible to Romans 10:13 "For whosoever shall call upon the name of the Lord shall be saved." Jesus did not say you might be saved, but you shall be.

Mary Jane, I heard you call on God to forgive you and come live in your heart and save you." "Yes," "Where is Jesus right now?" She said, "In heaven." He is, but where else is He?" She thought and said, "He is in my heart." According to that verse you are either saved or God is a liar. Which one?" Quickly she said, "I am saved. God cannot lie." "How did Jesus get in your heart?" "I asked in faith." "John 3:16 says, 'For God so loved the world that He gave His only begotten Son that whosoever should believe on Him shall not perish but have everlasting life.' According to that verse what kind of life do you have now?" After looking at the verse again she said, "Eternal life." "Who gave you eternal life?" "God." "Where are you going when you die?" "To Heaven." "Who says so?" "God." "Can He lie?" "No."

"Now Mary Jane, God wants to fill you with the Holy Spirit. Ephesians 5:18 says, 'Be filled with the Spirit'. You have the Holy Spirit in you now but you may not know it. Ask God in your prayer to fill you. He promises to fill you. He may want to see your faith before He does. Ask Him also to let you know you are going to heaven when you die. Man cannot let you know this but God can.

259

The only way you can grow as a Christian is to read your Bible (start with the Gospel of John in the New Testament) and pray. Keep God in your thoughts. Keep your mind on God. Think about Him all day and tell others what He has done for you. In Revelation 20:15 says, 'Whosoever's name is not found in the Book of Life is cast into the lake of fire.' When God calls the roll someday, you will answer. 'Yes, I'm here.' Your name has just been written in the Lamb's Book of Life."

IX

WHAT A WONDERFUL DAY!

Al tells of interesting happenings that took place in the years of 1987 and 1989. He said, "Our Liberty Flames baseball team traveled to the East Coast to play Old Dominion University. Bobby Richardson had become the baseball coach at Liberty University and I was the Athletic Director as well as the pitching coach.

When the game started, I noticed two young ladies who were ball girls for Old Dominion, sitting on a bench near our dugout. I walked over to them and asked if I could sit with them. Without any hesitation, they told me to sit down.

I then told them that the reason I wanted to sit with them was to tell them of God's simple plan of salvation. At that point, one of the girls said, "I almost went to your college." She also said that her father was a deacon.

During the fourth inning, two more girls came to replace the two with whom I had been speaking. I asked them if I could sit with them and they said yes. I then shared with them the plan of salvation. When I asked them to make a decision to accept Christ, both of them prayed asking Him to be their Savior.

In the seventh inning, another girl came to replace one of the two to whom I was talking. I repeated my story to her. She asked me to sit down. I prayed and asked Christ to become real to her. I wrote down all of their names and addresses so I could send them follow up material.

Jackie, one of the Diamond Girls tells her side of the story of what took place. "In the spring of 1987, during my junior year, I was working as a Diamond Girl at a baseball game against Liberty University. At the time if someone had told me that it was a Christian school, I would not have grasped what that meant, other than thinking that they were "good" people. As part of our responsibilities as batgirls we had to rotate from home to visitor

261

dugouts and the press box. During this particular game I was at the home dugout first. We commented that the coach for the visiting team was sitting and being very friendly with the girls at the other dugout. This was unusual to us because although we were used to players being friendly, the coaches were always focused on the game. When I rotated to Liberty's dugout, Coach Worthington sat down and began talking with me. It was a gloomy, chilly day and the game seemed to be taking forever, so I had plenty of time to talk to him. He was asking me questions about my life and myself and was warm and friendly. I remember him talking very boldly about Jesus. This was the first time that the gospel had been shared with me. I prayed with him and later received information from him about Jesus and salvation. Although I did not receive Jesus at that time, I do know that the Lord used him to plant a seed in my heart.

In my senior year of college, I did an internship in athletics at a local country club, which turned into a full-time position just before graduation. Little did I know at the time that the job came so easily because God had placed me there to meet one of the members, Jeff Overton. Jeff was a Liberty graduate and a former baseball manager for Coach Worthington. Shortly after we met, we began dating and I started attending church with him. For the first time I realized that the Bible and Jesus related to my life. The Holy Spirit began working in my heart as I asked many questions. Jeff shared his knowledge about Jesus and the Bible with me. The more I learned, the more I knew I needed Jesus. A few months before our wedding, I accepted Jesus as my Savior."

In thinking of all that took place at that time, Al said, "Two years later, Jeff Overton, a former equipment manager of mine at Liberty, came out to the ballpark. He had earned a law degree from Campbell College in North Carolina. He told me that some girls he knew had been witnessed to by someone from Liberty. He said the girls were students at the time at Old Dominion. I told Jeff that I was the one who witnessed to them and even sent literature to each of them. I said that I didn't know if they ever received the literature because I did not hear from them.

Jeff said that they did receive it. He mentioned that he was soon to be married. When he said goodbye and started walking away, I said, "Jeff, who are you going to marry?" He said, "One of the ball girls." I was totally shocked.

That fall, Jeff came back to Liberty to see a football game and brought his wife with him. What a wonderful day that was to see the girl who I had prayed with two years before and was now married to my former equipment manager."

Jackie Overton tells a postscript to this amazing story. She said, "Looking back on my life now I can see how God used many people and circumstances to protect me, share the Lord with me, and bring me to salvation. Fifteen years and five children later, I still stand in awe of God's goodness, grace, and mercy. I praise Him that my children have been raised in a Christian home, surrounded by many godly influences, and have had many privileges that I did not have. Thus far, four of the five have accepted Christ. As I continue to grow in my knowledge of His Word, I love to see Him at work in my life and in the lives of those around me. We serve an awesome God!"

X

AL SPEAKS FROM HIS HEART

"My desire for this book is to strengthen God's people in their walk with Him and help those who are lost to come to accept Christ as their Savior. One way to do that is to tell how sinful habits had a stronghold on my life.

In my story, I told how I started out in gambling by playing marbles as a boy. From that simple start grew a habit that could have destroyed my life. Gambling grows like a deadly cancer and eventually gets to the place where it cannot stop outside of a miraculous intervention by the Lord.

If you are in the grip of a deadly habit, my dear gambling friend, my heart goes out to you. Gambling had control of me more than anything in the world. I just could not stop. It is a terrible thing to know that you are caught in its web and cannot escape. Gambling had me where I was a helpless slave to it. I was totally consumed by it.

I shutter to think where I was hopelessly headed. Would I be the next gambling victim and lose my wife, children, home, and self-respect? I can't begin to describe the excitement that filled me to roll the dice, play poker, or bet on dog races.

In 1955, I went to Puerto Rico to play ball. I was drawn immediately like a magnet to the gambling places. My first night there, I won $500 at the hotel just across the street from our apartment. There, the government ran the gambling business. On my second trip to the hotel, I won another $500. I told my wife at that point that I didn't have to play baseball anymore for a living. I said that all I had to do was gamble for my income.

That second $500 was the last that I won. I immediately lost the $1,000. I then began to write IOU's slips for $100. I couldn't believe I was doing that but I couldn't help myself. I knew that I desperately needed help to free me from that horrible cancerous habit eating on me. My very existence was at stake. I did not have the answer.

Praise God, there was an answer and it was in the Lord. I turned to Him for salvation. He also cleaned up my life. I was miracously freed from the bonds of gambling. Since that wonderful event in my life, I have not been tempted to gamble even one time. When God sets us free, His Word tells us we are free indeed.

I never was a big drinker but its hold on lives is every bit as powerful as gambling. I did experience the frightening grip of smoking cigarettes but God freed me from that as well. What I want you to know, dear friend is that if you turn to Him for deliverance, He will free you from gambling, drinking, lying, cheating, smoking, or any sinful habits you might have. He will give you victory and put a song in your heart. What a difference God can make in your life if you turn to Him. He loves you and He is ready to help you.

XI

RADIATING THE LORD

Al returned to his hotel room in San Francisco one time to find his roommate watching television, which was the norm for him. Wanting to read his Bible and have a quiet time with the Lord, Al went into the bathroom and closed the door behind him! He sat down in the dry tub, which was somewhat comfortable.

After reading, singing, and praying for about 45 minutes, he went back into the room where his friend was watching television. He looked at his roommate and said, "If you would get saved, I would invite you to my prayer meeting." Of course, when that happens, we sure won't meet in the bathroom.

A short time later, Al's roommate came over to him and said, "Don't you know I can still see the love on the man's face and peace in his eyes?"

He was referring to a Christian man who came to the ball part in Cincinnati to talk with Al. Al's roommate was sitting in the bullpen when the stranger appeared from out of the stands. The man's look captivated Al's roommate. He couldn't get over the peaceful look the stranger had.

His roommate went on to say, "Can I be saved and still go to the church that I attend?" Al told him he didn't care what church he went to but would he come to Jesus Christ the way the Bible says that we should come to Him?

His roommate was faced with the truth of God's Word and turned away from it. As far as Al knew, his friend never came to Christ. His church meant more to him then coming to Christ for salvation.

XII

WITH INDIANAPOLIS

One morning I woke up in the Adolphus Hotel in Dallas, Texas, and I had my first and only pity party. It was a little rough at this time to be able to eat with some of the players after the games. I felt lonely and unloved but when I came across I John 1:3, my loneliness ended. God said, "...and truly our fellowship is with the Father, and his Son Jesus Christ." I have never been lonely since. Now I'm not saying I never will be again, but if ever I am my mind will go to this verse.

XIII

WITH THE GIANTS

When I let the Giants players know that I was saved I became very concerned. My first thought was I couldn't hold out. What would I do? After reading Philippians 1:6, I have rejoiced ever since. It says, "Being confident of this very thing, that he which hath begun a good work in you will perform it until the day of Jesus Christ." I do not have to hold out, Jesus is holding out for me. What a Great Joy!

HIGHLIGHTS OF AL WORTHINGTON'S ATHLETIC CAREER

The following is a statistical compilation of Al Worthington's athletic career, beginning with high school and ending with his years as Liberty University baseball coach. This information has been gathered and produced by the Liberty University Sports Information Department.

1944-1948 – Phillips High School, Birmingham, Alabama

Football

Voted All-State at end.
Selected to the coaches All-City team
Named Birmingham's Outstanding Lineman of the Year.
Team's Most Valuable Player

Track and Field

Finished second in the state in the shot put
Finished third in the state in the 120 high hurdles

At the end of Al's Phillips career he had won many awards. He was one of only four, four letter winners in the school's history. One sportswriter commented that Worthington was not only the best punter in the city, but also maybe the best in any city.

1948-1951 – Attended University of Alabama on a football scholarship.

Played football until a shoulder injury ends his career as a sophomore.

College pitching record – 14-2 including playoffs. 3-2 as a sophomore, 6-1 as a junior and 5-0 as a senior.

Appeared in the 1950 College World Series in Omaha during junior season. Pitched and lost to Washington State. Overall record in NCAA playoffs 2-1.

Southeastern Conference champions (1950)

Summer, 1950 – Pitched in Fulda (MN) Semi-Pro League, posting a 14-3 record.

Pitched one no-hitter and won first three games allowing just six total hits.

May 28, 1951- Signed professional contract with the Nashville Vols of the Southern League.

Won first professional game on June 1, 1951 over Birmingham Barons, 8-5.

Led team in shutouts with three.

1952 – Nashville Vols, Southern League (AA).

Final record was 13-13.

Led team in innings pitched (221), wins, strikeouts (152) and ERA (3.54).

Also led all of the Southern League in strikeouts.

Contract purchased by New York Giants after the1952 season.

1953 – Began season with the Minneapolis Millers.

July 3, 1953 – Called up to New York Giants: 25 months after leaving Alabama

July 6, 1953 – First major league start; 2-hit, 6-0 shutout of the Philadelphia Phillies. Six strikeouts.

July 11, 1953 – Second major league start; 4-hit, 6-0 shutout of the Brooklyn Dodgers. Seven strikeouts. It was the first time Brooklyn was shut out during the 1953 season.

First rookie in National League's modern era (46 years) to break in with consecutive shutouts.

Worthington's 6-0 shutout of Brooklyn on July 11 was the only time that Brooklyn was shutout that season. It also snapped Brooklyn's streak of consecutive games with one or more home runs at 24, one short of the major league record held by the New York Yankees.

1954 Began season with the Minneapolis Millers.
Was the top vote getter for the American Association All-Star game.
June 1954 – Called up to the New York Giants.

1955 – Spent the entire season with the Minneapolis Millers.
Named to the American Association's All-Star team.
Finished regular season with a 19-10 record, 17 complete games and 148 strikeouts. 3.58 ERA was also the lowest on the team.
Led AA in wins and complete games.
Led the Millers to their first ever Little World Series championship.
Worthington pitched in 10 of the 12 winning playoff games.
The millers did not lose a game, which Worthington appeared in during the playoffs.
The Millers were the first American Association team to win eight games in a row in the playoffs. Al pitched in six of the eight games.
In 1955, Worthington was named Minnesota's Outstanding Athlete of the Year.

In 1904 the Little World Series began between the American Association and the International League. Until 1955, Minneapolis had never gotten past the first round play-offs. In 1955, Minneapolis won 8 straight games. Al pitched in the first four and two out of the next four. During the best four out of seven series with Rochester in the Little World Series, Al won three games and saved the fourth. This had never been done before. In Nicollet Park, the home of the Millers, Al's record was 24-5.

1956 – New York Giants.

1957 – New York Giants.

1958 – San Francisco Giants

Finished with an 11-7 record and was the winningest right-hander on the team.

Traded to Boston Red Sox in April 1960.
1960 – Began season with Boston Red Sox. On April 15 he was sold to the Minneapolis Millers. September 1, he was sold to the Chicago White Sox. Spent six days with Chicago before quitting because they were stealing signals.

1961 – Played with San Diego in Triple A.
Pitched first no-hit, no-run game in the 25-year history of the Pacific Coast League in Westgate Park when he beat the Hawaii Islanders 5-0.
Put together a string of 27 consecutive scoreless innings in three straight nine-inning starts.

1962 – Played with the Indianapolis Indians in the American Association.
Finished with a team best 15-4 record and a 2.90 ERA.
Led team in innings pitched (217) and strikeouts (149).
Best winning percentage in the American Association and second best ERA.
American Association Champions.

1963 – Cincinnati Red
Season ERA was 3.00.

April 15, 1964 – Sent to San Diego in Triple A.
June 26, 1964 – Sold to the American League's Minnesota Twins.
Finished season with 5-6 record, 14 saves and a 1.38 ERA.
ERA was lowest of any reliever in the major leagues.
Did not allow an earned run in his first 20 appearances. Four earned runs given up in his first 30 games.
Selected as the Twins Pitcher of the Year.

1965 – Minnesota Twins
Finished regular season 10-7, with 13 saves and an ERA of 2.25.
Appeared in 59 regular season contests.

Helped Twins win the American League pennant before losing World Series to the Los Angeles Dodgers 4-3.
Selected as the Twins Pitcher of the Year.

1966- Minnesota Twins
Appeared in 65 games.
Finished with a 6-3 record, 11 saves and a 2.47 ERA.
Placed on Calvin Griffith's "Untouchable List."

1967 – Minnesota Twins
Appeared in 59 games.
Finished with an 8-9 record, 13 saves, and a 2.184 ERA.

1968 – Minnesota Twins
Appeared in 54 games.
Finished with an 8-9 record, 13 saves, and a 2.84 ERA.

1969 – Minnesota Twins
Appeared in 46 games.
Finished with a 4-1 record, three saves and a 4.57 ERA.

1972-1973 – Returned to Minnesota to serve as the teams pitching coach.
He inherited a pitching staff whose pitchers had a previous years ERA of 3.81.

In 1972 his staff set a Twins record for the lowest ERA that still stands at 2.84.

1973-1986 – Served as Liberty University's baseball coach for 13 seasons.

Career record was 343-191-1 (.641).

Had twelve seasons in which his teams won twenty or more games. Three times Liberty won at least 30 games and in 1983 they won 40 games.

Compiled a 14-13 record against Virginia Tech and the University of Virginia.

Appeared in three consecutive NAIA World Series (1981-83), finishing fifth in each appearance.

Had nine players drafted and given the opportunity to play professionally.

Upon retiring at the end of the 1986 season, Liberty's baseball complex was named "Worthington Field."

TWIN HIGHLIGHTS

As a Twin Al appeared in 327 games, winning 37 and saving 72. Al pitched when, as the 1972 Twins Yearbook stated, "a save was a save." Former Twins owner Calvin Griffith recently commented that in his 29 years as owner, from 1955 to 1984, Al was his number one pitcher during that time. On July 31, 1986, Worthington's years in Minnesota were rewarded when the Twins fans selected him as the Relief Pitcher of the Twins All-Time team. In the year 2000 Al was again elected to the Twins All-Time team as a relief pitcher. When his playing career ended, Al's ERA was 2.62, a club record for the lowest ERA. Worthington had five consecutive seasons in which he appeared in at least 40 games and had an ERA below 3.00.

MAJOR LEAGUE NOTES

Pitched in 602 games in his major league career, winning 79 games and posting a career ERA of 3.39 with 108 saves.

Appeared in 1,245 innings on six different teams.

ABOUT THE AUTHOR

V. Ben Kendrick, with his wife, Nina, has been actively involved in Missions since 1949. They served as missionaries in the Chad and Central African Republics in various capacities for 22 years. Dr. Kendrick later served in the administration of Baptist Mid-Missions for 20 years. His next step of service was to join the administration of Heritage Baptist University in Greenwood, Indiana, where he teaches Missions and is Vice President of Advancement. He has served two colleges as trustee for a total of 22 years. Dr. Kendrick has authored eight books and has had over 1,000 articles published. As for his limited baseball background, he is listed in his high school Hall of Fame, played some semi-pro ball, and attended two St. Louis Cardinals tryout camps. Dr. and Mrs. Kendrick have three children.

Printed in the United States
25536LVS00005B/1-51

9 781594 677885